North Shore

a collection of poems

by

Herbert Merrill

NORTH SHORE was assembled by the author, **Herbert Merrill**, edited and transcribed by **Kathleen Merrill**, with suggested additions by **Virginia Merrill Wilson**. The vast majority of the poems have been previously published from the late 1940's to the early 1960's in various national magazines.

North Shore: A Collection of Poems by Herbert Merrill

COPYRIGHT 2020: Kathleen Merrill

All rights are reserved. No part of this book may be used or reproduced in any manner whatsoever without written permission of the editor, Kathleen Merrill, except in the case of brief quotations embodied in critical articles or reviews.

Front Cover art: Kathleen Merrill. Photo: Artist Point, Lake Superior

Vintage head shot photo: Sergeant Herbert Merrill, circa 1944, provided by Virginia Merrill Wilson

First Edition

Print ISBN 9798646907654

Published in the United States of America

To the loving memory of

Herbert James Merrill

1915-1995

Tribute

From his poems, you'd think he was a farmer born to rocky soil and daily toil, but in fact, our father hailed from Chicago, son to a design engineer and grandson to a high school principal. He grew up with books and ideas, but spent all his free time outside. He had a lifelong love affair with the land, the lakes, the mountains, sky and sea. His relationship to nature was almost like a religion.

From his poems, you'd think him intimate with all manner of animals—wild and domestic, but in fact, our father, while a dedicated observer of all creatures furred and feathered, owned only dogs and the occasional cat that curled in his lap while he wrote. He taught his two daughters to recognize birds and birdsong, to identify insects and lake critters, encouraged them to be aware and nurtured by the natural universe.

From his poems, you'd think he was a passionate husband who tragically lost the love of his life way too soon, and you'd be right. As a single dad, he raised his young girls to adulthood, instilling in them a certainty that they could do anything they wanted in this world, giving them the gift of confidence while blanketed in the safety of his love.

We thank you.

The Poems

North Shore	1
Becalmed	2
Near Miss	3
Crossing the Ice	4
Lake Change	5
November Beach	6
The Winter Fishing	7
Star Voyage	8
The Summer Lake	9
Along Shore	10
Low Tide	11
September Sail	12
Night Swim	13
Reflections on a Pond	14
A Bowl of Stars	15
Evening Song	16
The Gentle Days	17
Spring Voyage	18
Lost Rivers	19
Bean Blossom Pond	20
The Scrub Oak Tree	21
Night Song	22
Rail Fence	23
On the Apple Wagon	24
Ridge Wind	25
Captive	26
One Hill from Heaven	27
Mid-Winter Lament	28
Farm Gone	29
The Sorry Sun	30
November Jail-Break	31
Snow Fence	32
The Coming On	33
Burned Out	34
Windy Weather	35
Burning Leaves	36
The Winter Heart	37
April Evening	38
First Acquaintance	39
Lullaby	40
Songs at Evening	41
Night Fears	42

Two in the Sun	43	Starlight Abandoned	63
The Sleepy Time	44	Tin Roof	64
Grandpa Sleeping	45	Long Night	65
By Lamplight	46	Long Legs	66
Star Child	47	In the Garden	67
Bone Weary	48	Morning Song	68
On the Porch	49	Crow	69
The Snub	50	Tabby by Day, Tabby by Dark	70
Cobb's Defeat	51	Weather Vane	71
Night Thoughts on Christmas Eve	52	Beech in the Wind	72
My Neighbor John	53	Train at Night	73
Visiting	54	Thanksgiving Sonnet	74
Swamp Turtle	55	Imprisoned Spring	75
Stars and a Frog	56	Cicada	76
Wabash Catfish	57	Brown Winter	77
Mr. Bumpy	58	Time Song	78
June Bug	59	View Shift	79
Copperhead	60	Fire Fall	80
Closed Shop	61	Summer Sleep	81
The Wayward Hen	62		

Sunrise on Wheels	82
Fire by Night	83
The Night Watch	84
Caleb and the Frogs	85
Stray Pine	86
Objection	87
Salamander	88
Sun	89
Going Back	90
Sun in the Morning	91
Subway Soliloquy	92
Cleaning Lady	93
The Winter Harbor	94
My Urban Aunt	95
Miss Mattie	96
Allegheny Front	97
River Worry	98
Old Riddle	99
The Planting	100
Magic	101
Winter Memory	102
Kite Time	103
The Cottagers	104
Ditch Diggers	105
Chris Swenson	106
Elvira Ball	107
Sarah Hall	108
Tim Bacon	109
Doc Preston	110
Old Gettels	111
Empido's Swamp	112
Morning by Windy Hill	113
Donnegan's Notion	114
Wasps	115
Scarecrow	116
Back Country	117
Fawn	118
Mouse	119
New Day	120

The Gifts	121	Winter Weary	141
Giant Sleeping	122	Sudden Shower	142
Wind and Fire	123	April	143
Easter Parade	124	Sun Sitter	144
Sundown	125	Polar Expedition	145
Witch Trouble	126	Tom in the Woods	146
Midwinter	127	Let Me Back In	147
White Magic	128	Keeping Warm	148
Abigail	129	Two-Footed Puzzle	149
November Song	130	Autumn Apology	150
Autumn Protest	131	Scene Shift	151
Mare Apparent	132	Bright Moment	152
Drought	133	Hospital Nursery	153
After the Ball	134	Highway Report	154
Buzzard	135	Possum Country	155
Rainy Easter	136	Windfall of Robins	156
Storm Cellar	137	Time Was	157
February Sun	138	June Check-Up	158
Mending Days	139	Late Comer	159
North Wind	140	Making My Peace	160

Anniversary	161
Post Office Spring	162
Windjammer	163
Hidden Fire	164
Pete	165
Friend in Need	166
Footpace	167
Spring Flight	168
Outside and In	169
Baking Day	170
Well-Mannered	171
Now Playing	172
Boy Trap	173
May Morning	174
Two Miracles	175
Advent	176
The Backward Look	177
Going Away	178
Color Time	179
Night Walk	180
The Treasure Field	181
The Buckler And the Blade	182
By the Fire	183
Night Self	184
Winter Carpentry	185
Second Chorus	186
Cold Reception	187
Autumn Appraisal	188
Man Versus Housekeeping	189
Winter Woods	190
Visionary	191
First Comer	192
Going Back	193
The Defense Rests	194
The Web of Frost	195
Time to Go In	196
The Sleepers And the Sun	197
Midsummer Night Christmas	198

Two-Legged Year	199	The Fragile Time	218
Complaint Department	200	Better Come In	219
Thanksgiving Cup	201	Nativity	220
Witch	202	An Old Song For a New Year	221
Disturbing the Peace	203	Valentine	222
Status Quo	204	Spring Fires	223
Late Lake	205	Morning After Storm	224
Stubborn	206	First Picnic	225
Summer Midnight	207	Sky Bull	226
Forsaken Lane And Empty Church	208	The Rooster And the Sun	227
The Sleepy Dance	209	Rain Loose	228
Midnight Zero	210	The Broken Night	229
Time Bomb	211	Deep Summer	230
The Springtime Pig	212	Windy Summit	231
A Northern View	213	The Robin Tree	232
Launching Platform	214	The Trap	233
Star Swing	215	Generally Speaking	234
Moon Walking	216	Kathy	235
In the Hayfield	217	Hall of Giants	236

Courthouse Square	237
Thick Tonight	238
Mountain Farm	239
Ethan Benderby	240
Pumpkin Time	241
Spring Morning	242
Firewood	243
Involuntary	244
The Quiet Answer	245
In the Hayloft	246
Mole	247
Sound Track	248
Crisis Averted	249
Empty Woodchuck	250
The Flower Eater	251
Elbow Room	252
The Winter Crop	253
In the Doorway	254
Recital	255
Thaw	256
A Carol For Two Voices	257
City: Day's End	258
New Lamb in March	259
Black Angus	260
Love Song	261
The Watcher	262
Deep-Rooted	263
October Meeting	264
The End of It	265
Home by Starlight	266
Dark Visitor	267
Spring Questioning	268
My Love and I	269
Requiem	270
Sky Cottage	271
Search for the Sun	272
Alone Awake	273
Acceptance	274
Timber Patch	275

Old Earth	276
Queen's Gambit Refused	277
A Stony Field	278
Pear Tree	279
Unwilling Traveler	280
High Swallow	281
Moss Hartman	282
Winter Thunder	283
Snow Fire	284
The Search	285
The Magic Patch	286
A Special Joy	287
The Coming In	288
Rock Ridge Elegy	289
Music Lover	290
Star Lost	291
Gray Lace	292

North Shore

Earth closes here with nothing more to say.
It speaks a final leaf and then gives way
Entirely to the silent sea and sky,
The only comment now a gull's cold cry
Or spent waves whispering upon the sand
In soft astonishment at touching land.
A thousand miles away, when I was young,
Each flower spoke a colored word, each tongue
Of summer grass a reassuring phrase.
The nights were loud with stars, and all the days
Sang with the yellow music of the sun.
But that was long ago, and I for one
Welcome the silence now and, even more,
The harsh integrity of this far shore.

———

Becalmed

Well, there I was and there I stuck,
A helpless victim of the weather,
My little boat a sitting duck
Without a wind to stir a feather.
Her sail hung limply down like two
White, withered petals in the sun;
The lake was like a pot of glue,
The skipper like a hot-cross bun.
And all the yellow afternoon,
A fly upon a windowpane,
I buzzed and grumbled till the moon
Replaced a sunset's crimson stain
And took me home with breezes stirring
As gently as a kitten's purring.

                    The Saturday Evening Post

Near Miss

I shoved off into fog at dawn,
And in three paddle strokes the mist
Had closed upon me like a fist,
And all familiar things were gone.
I saw the silver cage of rain,
The dripping blade, the sullen flood,
And finally looming red as blood,
The buoy that marked the shipping lane.
I heard the freighter then, a blind
Heavy-throated crying sound,
And felt a heavy swell and found
Terror at my heart and mind,
As death himself emerged from a cloud
And passed me in his iron shroud.

Crossing the Ice

Between the frozen lake and sky
There moves a solitary speck,
A curious, two-legged I
Pacing the winter's quarter-deck.
Caught between immensities,
Neither of which I understand,
I watch the blue infinities
That yawn above the edge of land;
Then downward bow my head to stare
Through windows of clear ice. My breath
Curls like a question mark in air,
As I tread softly over death
And see him wait below the thin
Pane that will not let me in.

Saturday Evening Post, January 18, 1958 p.73

Lake Change

Only a handful of weeks ago
The lake was a living, restless thing,
With whitecaps running row on row
And sailboats racing wing to wing.
The little children in the sand,
The bittern on the fallen tree,
The fisherman who waved his hand,
All seemed so permanent to me.
And yet I know what all men know:
Time had to close the iron vise,
And sails of canvas turn to snow
Ghosting along the midnight ice.
Orion has no choice. He must
Scuffle his boots in white stardust.

November Beach

The cottagers have gone away
And left the lake a quiet place.
Of all the boats that stirred the bay
There is no trace.
The little houses on the beach
Are locked and boarded up so tight
That even now, at noontime, each
Is filled with night.
A single pair of seagulls talk
Along the edge of lake and land,
And print a pattern where they walk
Of stars in sand.
And I, too, walk along the shore,
But leave a clumsy, human track
That ties me fast to my own door
When I look back.

The Winter Fishing

Five fathoms underneath this sheet
Of green lake ice on which I stand
The pike patrols his timeless beat,
Gliding above the tawny sand.
The head is a rigid brutal mask,
The body a blade with fluted fin,
And both are made for a single task
Of feeding the hunger caged within.
I take my spudding tool and chip
A circle into liquid night,
The line runs in my mitten's grip,
The silver minnow glitters bright,
Till suddenly the great jaws snap
And death is lunging on a string.
I haul him up and watch my trap
Freeze again to an opaque ring.

The Saturday Evening Post, January 30, 1954, p.83

Star Voyage

It was sometime between midnight and dawn,
Someplace between a mile and two from shore,
Out where the bottom shoals up and is gone
Down deep again to eighty feet or more.
And there I had been fishing, all serene,
Until I saw the stars come down to float
Into the quiet water. Gold and green
They swam into the darkness underneath the boat.
I lifted up my eyes and saw the cool
White flowers growing in the field of night,
And down I looked to see them like a school
Of living minnows in a lake of light.
And all night long, my rod upon my knees,
I drifted, fishing in the Pleiades.

―――

The Saturday Evening Post, September 4, 1948, p.56

The Summer Lake

All day long in a blaze of heat
Under a white and empty sky
The lake lay flat as a metal sheet
Forged on the anvil of July.
One gull troubled the quiet air
And far below one ripple rolled
Over the sandy shallows where
A garfish swam in liquid gold.
At last the sun with a scarlet yawn
Strolled downhill to another place,
And blessed darkness came till dawn
Lifted a pale and sleepy face.
But all night long the lake had been
Cooled by the light of a curving moon
That dappled the water's dusky skin
And stirred the waves with a silver spoon.

———

The Saturday Evening Post, July 16, 1955 p.48

Along Shore

There is no wind to mar the fine
Unblemished surface of the sea,
Nor any sort of warning sign
To trouble it or trouble me.
And yet the waters rise in slow
Compulsive swells along the shore,
To mutter of the long ago
And whisper of the nevermore.
There is no fury in me now
This evening, as I come to stand
And watch the tired breakers bow
White heads before the waiting land,
But still I feel their counterpart
Within my own unquiet heart.

The Saturday Evening Post, November, 1960

Low Tide

The dunes are curled like cats asleep.
Between their paws the breakers run.
The clouds are grazing, calm as sheep,
Over the pastures of the sun.
I walk upon infinity,
A moving dot on the yellow sand,
Between the age-old trinity
Of shoreless sky and sea and land.
And all that marks my passing there,
As far as anyone can tell,
Is pipe smoke left upon the air
And footprints for the tide to fill.

―――――

The Saturday Evening Post, June 4, 1949, p.65

September Sail

I sailed these waters long ago
When I was seventeen or so,
On such another autumn night
As this, the ghosting wind as light
The same old frosty moon afloat,
And everywhere around the boat,
Above my masthead and below.
A drift of stars like fallen snow.
It's all the same as once before
From sky to lake and shore to shore,
And yet inexplicably changed:
The pattern slightly rearranged,
The wind a little colder somehow,
The stars a little older now.

The Saturday Evening Post, 1961

Night Swim

Lapped in a wave from toe to chin,
I shed the hot day like a skin
And swam into the heart of night
To share the darkness with moonlight.
I turn and float, my body buoyed
Up in a blue and star-hung void,
And there like a naked soul I lie
Between deep-fathomed lake and sky.
Then in a breath, my blood runs cold,
Infinite is the night and old,
But I a dangling puppet thing
Held by a star on a silver string,
Caught by the moon in a silver mesh
With arms of water around my flesh,
Till, twisting from the dark embrace,
I swim for the lamp-lit landing place.

———

The Saturday Evening Post, July 11, 1953, p.93

Reflections on a Pond

The pond is an unwinking eye
Staring always at the sky,
Golden with the sun at noon,
Silvered by the midnight moon.
Yet in heaven and beyond
Not a thing reflects the pond.

I too contemplate the sun,
Count the planets, one by one,
In my heart absorb the light,
And scan the sky in vain to see
Mirrored there the likes of me.

A Bowl of Stars

Tonight the lake is like a sky
So full of swimming stars that I
No longer can be certain where
The boundaries are of earth and air.
I see with something of a shock
A full moon anchored by the dock
And note the dipper floating up
With water spilling from its cup.
About the most that I can be
Quite sure of is that I am me,
Standing here upon the sand,
Attached by both my feet to land,
But staring with a puzzled frown
At what might well be up or down.

Evening Song

A summer twilight drowses on the lake,
The quiet water sleeps beside the shore,
A single muskrat leaves a silver wake,
Sculling himself along with silent oar,
And I hear music rising, frail and thin,
Where cattails lift a cage of rusty bars
And one small marsh wren tunes his violin,
Perhaps to serenade a flight of stars.
How many summer evenings I have seen
Settle themselves to rest upon this place
Where sky and water meet along a green
Selvedge of grass and trees. I pray some trace
Of their tranquility I may hold fast
When evening comes upon me too at last.

———

The Gentle Days

On mornings when the wind lay half asleep
Dreaming a summer dream upon the lake,
Stirring in slumber now and then to make
A riffling, when the clouds like shaggy sheep
Grazed on the water, mirrored in the deep,
And one gull dozed upon the mooring stake:
On such a morning you and I would take
A doll, a dog, a fishing pole, and creep
Off on a voyage in the slow sailboat,
Ourselves a dream, a summer dream afloat,
With doll clothes in the rigging, hung to dry
Beneath a sun that watched with golden eye,
The old dog sleeping and yourself a child.
How long ago—those days that gently smiled.

Spring Voyage

Beware, my little boat, the swift
Tidal race where breakers drift
Soft as foaming clouds above
Rocks as sharp as broken love.

Carry me, I pray, as far
As the island of a star:
Catch the wind of Time and make
Heaven but a furrowed wake.

Lift a swelling, silver wing
Take me to eternal spring,
And if we founder in our flight
Bear me deep below the night.

Lost Rivers

Here in the limestone country, rivers rise
Right up out of a rock before your eyes
And disappear in earth like an oak root
To search out caves beneath a mountain's foot.
I've heard them guess, but no one ever found
Where these deep waters go underground—
Whether they fountain out in springs, to spill
Their shining ribbons down a far-off hill,
Or grow upright into green leaves of corn,
Or jet like music from some mountain horn.

The Saturday Evening Post, July 16, 1949, p.89

Bean Blossom Pond

They dammed Bean Blossom Creek to make
A field of water with green shores
Where cottonwood and sycamores
Can stretch their wrists above the lake
And wet their crooked finger tips.
Crouching humpbacked ridges lie
Between blue water and blue sky
And lap the pond with sandy lips.

I've never found a better place
To fish for perch with orange fins,
Or pumpkinseeds with copper skins,
Or black bullhead with whiskered face,
Or just to drift without a purpose,
Leaving the colored string uncaught,
To watch a slowly swimming thought
Come rising up to break the surface.

―――

The Saturday Evening Post, April 28, 1951, p.121

The Scrub Oak Tree

Some twenty years ago an acorn dropped
Into a rocky place, where limestone showed
A few white teeth and where the forest stopped
Before the red slash of a quarry road.
It had no business to be hatching there,
Splitting the brown egg shell and thrusting out
A skinny leg of green life on the bare
Inhospitable ledge. A week, no doubt,
Would see it shrivel up and starve itself,
A pinch of failure in a cup of stone.
But there it stands today upon its shelf,
Its talons in the rock. I freely own
The whole thing baffles me, and I can show
Statistics proving that it couldn't grow.

———

Night Song

Dark mother night and cool, white-handed moon,
Come gently to me now, I pray, come soon
And hold me in your arms of velvet dark
As closely as a tree is held in bark.
Let there be shadows spread upon the ground
So soft that I can hear the earth go round,
And from a far-off, singing steeple send
A flight of silver bells to mark day's end.
Be my physician and my cure in one,
And heal these eyes half-blinded by the sun.
Give me a bowl of stars, a cup of night,
To be my diet and my heart's delight,
And one high hill where I can sit and see
The world in God's great hand sleep quietly.

———

The Saturday Evening Post, April 15, 1950, p.119

Rail Fence

The fence comes out of an alder wood
And zigzags halfway up the hill.
Nobody knows how long it's stood,
But everyone says it's a good fence still.
Four inches wide from edge to edge
With scarcely any warp at all,
Walnut split with an iron wedge
By a steady hand on the hickory maul.

The only trouble, there's nothing to fence;
Only a squirrel or a hopping crow.
Nothing at all that it still prevents
From getting out or in. There's no
Need any more for its silver rails,
Except for the sun to touch with gold,
Or robins to sit on and sing their scales,
Or morning- glories to catch and hold.

The Saturday Evening Post, August 27, 1949

On the Apple Wagon

You dropped it? Well, we've plenty and to spare.
What's one red apple lost from such a load?
Someone will come along and find it there,
And wonder how it happened on the road
So far from apple trees. He'll turn it round
In his two hands and shine it on his coat,
Bite in at last and find an apple sound
And fit to cool a dusty tongue or throat.
Or if it rolled off into the tall grass
To make a bottom for a bladed well,
Some bird will use it for a drinking glass
Or drunken bees will stagger in its shell,
Or likely it will vanish in one bite
Inside a cow come swaying home tonight.

The Saturday Evening Post, August 28, 1948, p.53

Ridge Wind

High on the ridge's bony back
When lights are off and night is black,
The wind is a toothless, talking sound,
Mumbling secrets to the ground
Or crying in the brittle grass
Or whispering by the window glass,
And over and over again each night
Whistling tunes that won't come right,
An off-key, dissonant, sighing strain
That starts and stops and starts again.
But when the sunup's golden eye
Opens wide on earth and sky,
And morning arches its blue bridge
A thousand miles above the ridge,
The wind becomes a mighty thing
That beats the air with giant wing
And makes the pine tree cry aloud
And creams the heaven up with cloud.

―――――

The Saturday Evening Post, January 7, 1950, p.86

Captive

One day I walked among the corn to see
Whether the silk had started turning red,
And quietly the field closed in on me
Like some green ocean, higher overhead
Than I could reach, and everywhere around
The waves of green went rolling far and near.
The green stalks marched beside me on the ground,
A million green leaves rustled in my ear,
And corridors of green half-light stretched thin
Before me and behind and all about,
Until I turned and found myself hemmed in
By vertical green bars with no way out,
And for an hour there that seemed an age
I paced, a captive, in a great green cage.

The Saturday Evening Post, August 14, 1948, p.60

One Hill from Heaven

A hillside led me up today
Toward heaven through a field of hay,
While sunlight spread a yellow hand
Upon my head and on the land,
And grasshoppers jumped all around
When my boot heel would strike the ground.
I climbed until I reached the crown
And caught my breath and laid me down
Upon a scatter rug of shade
A tree obligingly had made.
There lifted heaven, farther still
Than I could reach beyond my hill,
And so I failed another time…
But there are higher hills to climb.

———

The Saturday Evening Post, May 13, 1950, p.132

Midwinter Lament

Oh, I am shuddering sick of sleet,
Fed to my chattering teeth with snow,
Tired to death of ten below,
And weary of rubber-booted feet.
I crave July with a lover's lust,
Covet sun with a miser's greed,
Long for a yellow noon, and need
The barefoot feel of summer dust.

———

The Saturday Evening Post, January 28, 1961, p.67

Farm Gone

How could I ever hope to find the place
The way it used to be? The city's grown
And swallowed up the farm without a trace.
Plain foolishness in me. I should have known
There'd be a rusty drainage pipe around
The chuckling creek, and layers of concrete
Six inches thick upon the buried ground,
And where the crooked cow path was, a street
For taxicabs to bustle up and down.
I'm sorry now that I came here to find
A boyhood memory in this iron town.
It's better to go back inside the mind
Where men are certain of the things they've got,
Not hunt for cows among the trolley cars,
Or pear trees in a crowded parking lot,
Or country ghosts below the neon stars.

―――

The Saturday Evening Post, October 14, 1950, p.71

The Sorry Sun

You'd think a sun that glows like fire
Would make the icicles perspire,
Loosen up the pond or whittle
Down a snowdrift's size a little,
Or, if nothing further, it
Might warm a body up a bit.
But not this sun, this withered rose,
That hangs there like a drunkard's nose
And burns away to no avail,
No hotter than a firefly's tail.
For all the good it does we might
As well depend on cold moonlight
Or lift our hands to warm them by
The North Star's glittering blue eye.

———

The Saturday Evening Post, January 5, 1952, p.62

November Jailbreak

I stopped this morning to admire
A row of icicles in sun
And watched prismatic colors run
About them like a restless fire,
Where bars of silver, cold and bright,
Had caged a leaping flame of light.

But by this noon the spell was gone
Only the gutter's iron lip
And water's rusty, measured drip
Gossiped of that imprisoned dawn
And hinted that tonight would make
Another jail for day to break.

The Saturday Evening Post, November 20, 1954, p.151

Snow Fence

When summer fills the valley's cup
These scarlet pickets are rolled up
To make red bundles in the clover
That fat, sun-drowsy cows graze over.
But when October snaps with cold,
The scarlet pickets are unrolled
And fastened upright in a row
To make a stand against the snow.
You might think only fools would try
Holding back the winter sky
With fragile spider webs of wood,
But you'd be wrong, and if I could
I'd fence myself about to keep
Time from drifting me too deep.

———

The Saturday Evening Post, December, 1960

The Coming On

When winter closes in
And haystacks brim with mice,
The river's wrinkled skin
Becomes a hide of ice,
The blizzard tries his teeth
On tattered garden plot,
And smoke displays a wreath
On every chimney pot.

The world's a frozen clod
And life a sealed cocoon,
The midnight sky a pod
That holds a withered moon;
A wind blows off the pole
And drives the bear to den,
The woodchuck to his hole,
And me indoors again.

The Saturday Evening Post, December 3, 1955, p.62

Burned Out

The chimney stands up all alone,
Naked without a house to hide it.
Nothing left but fire-scarred stone,
Weeds on a hearth and birds inside it.

What man lived here no man knows.
It's been a lifetime boarded up.
Mark how the poison sumac grows
Out of the cellar's sunken cup.

And see the old crab-apple trees,
Broken and bent and silver gray,
With gnarled elbows and stiffened knees.
Can't say I like it. Come away.

Best leave it to the prying root,
The fingers of the rain and sun,
The grackle's beak and mouse's foot
To end what fire has begun.

The Saturday Evening Post, June 10, 1950, p.150

Windy Weather

The west wind swaggers up the hill
To bang the shutters on the sill
And boot the scarecrow from his stick
And lend the Leghorn hen a kick.
He blows the wooden shingles off
And water from the water trough,
Red apples from the quaking tree,
And my own wind right out of me.
But while I grant he's rowdy rough,
I like the bully well enough.

What chills my blood and turns me old
Is a fish-wet east wind, gray and cold,
That laps the roots of apple trees
And breathes a fog upon my knees,
That sucks away the summer leaves
And sighs along the dripping eaves,
That creeps in every seam and crack
To run cold fingers down my back,
And wails as sadly as a mourner
Crying in a drafty corner.

The Saturday Evening Post, September 9, 1950, p.150

Burning Leaves

I heaped up leaves enough to make
A fire of all that fell today,
And stood there, leaning on a rake,
To watch the summer burn away.

The months curled upward, thick and blue,
And drifted off upon the breeze;
I saw the autumn turn into
A wraith of smoke upon the trees.

I watched the year by firelight
Until the flames were nearly gone;
Then in the first cold breath of night
I felt the winter coming on.

Stars glittered down like flakes of snow,
The fire guttered out and died,
And when a wind began to blow,
I shivered once and went inside.

The Saturday Evening Post, September 11, 1948, p.156

The Winter Heart

My heart, I grant the snow is deep,
The bushes look like shaggy sheep.
A yard of ice has crushed the pond,
And blizzards lie in wait beyond
The heavy gray horizon, where
A nimbus hangs in freezing air.
But I remind you, heart, that spring,
Though now a half-forgotten thing,
Is not a myth, nor yet a lie,
And even winter must go by.
So rouse up now and start to beat,
The seeds are there beneath my feet,
And once the sunlight brims in flood
The whole earth will begin to bud.

―――

The Saturday Evening Post, February 8, 1957

April Evening

Come sit outside awhile tonight
And help me taste this balmy weather.
We'll brim our eyes up with starlight
And hear the new leaves talk together.
Winter is the time for slumber,
Sealing up both earth and eye,
But now star flowers without number
Spill their blossoms on the sky.
And we'll stay up awhile to watch
The moon fly like a golden bee,
And smell the new-turned garden patch,
And feel the warm south wind and see
The poplar, tall and feather thin,
Brush winter out and April in.

―――

The Saturday Evening Post, April 7, 1951, p.59

First Acquaintance

You know, I had forgotten
How tiny babies are,
The nose a tender button,
The hand a fragile star.

A maple leaf might hide her
Or serve her for a dress.
Our three-year-old beside her
Seems like a giantess.

And when I bend above her,
It's like a mountain quaking.
I scarcely dare to love her
For fear of something breaking.

―――――

The Saturday Evening Post, April 21, 1951, p.179

Lullaby

Hushaby, hushaby, save your bright tears,
Save them to spend over all the long years.
Wait till you find a cause worthy of sorrow,
Not tonight, not tonight, nor yet tomorrow.

Hushaby, hushaby, gather them up,
Hide them away in your heart for a cup.
Tears are like silver, alas, when they're gone.
Save them to spend later on, later on.

Hushaby, hushaby, slumber is brief,
Morning will waken the flower and the leaf,
Time will be turning the dark into day,
Sleep awhile, little one, sleep while you may.

The Saturday Evening Post, May 21, 1949, p.138

Songs at Evening

The soft gray summer rain is done,
Departed is the creamy cloud.
Now at dusk, a red-checked sun
Watches a redbreast singing loud.

Here at the window, robin wings
And robin music flash my way:
And, rising on an echo, sings
The voice of my own child at play.

In rain-wet grass she skips along,
Piping in wordless joy to be
Caught in the rain of robin song
That showers down from every tree.

Like silver flute and golden bell,
I hear their song lift heavenward
Till my own heart begins to swell
And sings as loud as child or bird.

The Saturday Evening Post, August 19, 1950, p.98

Night Fears

When night is standing ceiling deep
Within the house and all is still,
I hear the child cry out in sleep
And call my name and call until
My eyelids lift upon the night,
And suddenly in strange dismay
I come awake and grope for light
And hear the child a room away.

Then in the cradle of my arms,
The curious fright and sleepy tear
And all the shadowy, vague alarms
Are rocked away and disappear.
To and fro and to and fro
Until a child sleeps tranquilly
And I remember long ago
Someone did the same for me.

———

The Saturday Evening Post, November 18, 1950, p.132

Two in the Sun

We have been friends for such a spell
That we don't talk much anymore.
He had his say out years before,
And I've told all I plan to tell.

It would be stranger now to hear
Him chatter than a talking tree,
And he would take it ill of me
To wag my clapper in his ear.

And so we sit and take the sun,
Together warming up our bones,
And quiet as a pair of stones
We let the blessed silence run.

―――

The Saturday Evening Post, September 26, 1953, p.61

The Sleepy Time

When I was a child in my father's house
With bedtime coming on apace,
I'd creep as quiet as any mouse
Over the rug to a secret place.

Under the table, or back of a chair
Or crannied behind the couch I'd lie
To hear the big folks talking there
And watch the shoes go walking by.

My mother's voice was a silver bird
That flew with a flutter of silver wings;
My father's laugh was the thunder stirred,
My sister's the ripple of sweet harp strings.

And while I stared through closing eyes,
Their words would buzz inside my head
Until I'd wake with a slow surprise
To find it morning and me in bed.

———

The Saturday Evening Post, May 23, 1953, p.162

Grandpa Sleeping

Beside the southern wall he sat and slept,
His closed eyes tilted upward to the sun,
Until the light waned and the shadows crept
Softly across the garden, one by one,
To run at last up both his legs, like mice,
And wake him with a nibbling of chill.
Then he'd get up and mutter once or twice
To see the sun go down behind the hill,
And, yawning loud and shaking his white head,
Would stamp indoors and up the stairs to bed.

The Saturday Evening Post, December 11, 1948, p.155

By Lamplight

When all the house is dark but for my light,
And all the world outside is wrapped in night,
And a black wind mutters and the stars are gone,
And dry leaves drag their bones across the lawn,
Then I can hear time rustling his wings
Beyond the little cone of lamplight things;
The memories come again: my mother's face,
The half-lost years, the half-forgotten place,
The boy I used to be, a stranger to me now;
For men, like locusts, shed their skins somehow
And change, outside and in, beyond returning
Except by night, with only one lamp burning.

―――

The Saturday Evening Post, My 10, 1952, p.151

Star Child

The child looks up into the night
To see the flowers of lovely light
And lifts a hand with fingers curled
To grasp the blossoms of a world.

She has not learned that it's too far
For us to touch a petaled star
Or stretch ourselves on tiptoe up
To pluck an astral buttercup.

And I shall never tell her so
But pray instead that she may go
On reaching all her lifetime through
Until she picks a star or two.

Bone-Weary

I am so tired tonight that my bones ache
And I could spend forever in this chair.
If I were martyred, tied up to a stake,
I'd sleep until the fire reached my hair.
If I were stretched out on a hill of ants,
I'd lie and let them chew with never a moan.
If Aphrodite dropped in for a dance,
I'd have to tell her to go dance alone.
I wish I had the strength to lift my head
And blow away the fly upon my nose,
Or shed my clothes and stagger into bed
And snore until I break the glass windows,
Or even to declare myself stone dead
And let my friends arrange for my repose.

The Saturday Evening Post, November 28, 1953, p.123

On the Porch

There's some that like the day and some the dark.
Your grandma now would sit there on the swing
At sundown, when the sleepy meadowlark
Runs down the scale, too drowsy most to sing,
And the robin uses up a few last notes.
She'd stay there on the porch all night, I guess,
If I'd have let her, watching how the oats
Lay silver in the moon, smoothing her dress,
Rocking back and forth. "Bedtime," I'd say;
"Sunup soon, and lots of work in sight."
Then she'd come in. Now me, I like the day.
A man can't cut a field by candlelight,
And sun is money saved, this time of year.
But grandma liked the dark…while she was here.

———

The Saturday Evening Post, August, 1948

The Snub

When I passed her on the street today
And smiled as usual and said good morning,
She cut her sharp eyes at me without warning,
And stabbed me through and through and went her way.
She left me there, my smile upon my face,
To watch her straight, uncompromising back
Go marching off inside its coat of black;
I put my smile away as out of place,
But what I've ever done to cause it all,
Or what I've ever said to rouse her blood,
Or what I've ever thought but to her good,
I cannot for the life of me recall.
And though she seemed deliberate, it might be
Merely a random shot that murdered me.

The Saturday Evening Post, February 19, 1949, p.44

Cobb's Defeat

Cobb had a valley run to seed
With burdock, wort and chicory,
Bouncing Bet and ironweed,
Yarrow, scoke, and blackberry,
Hardpan clay and stone and sand,
Mullein stalk and blue bull thistle.
All the meat worn off the land
And nothing left but bone and gristle.

Cobb, he said he'd had enough.
What use to plow and pay a tax
And get a crop of sorry stuff
Like cuckoo-buttons or toadflax?
"I'll quit," he said, "I'll let it choke
On partridge pea and milkweed fuzz,
Or knotweed, bur and poison oak."

And so he did, and so it does.

———

The Saturday Evening Post, July 22, 1950, p.102

Night Thoughts on Christmas Eve

The Christmas tree, the whispering fire and I
Are keeping midnight company with the deep,
Blue night outside and the star-seeded sky.
The wooden cuckoo clock has shrilled its cry
A dozen times and muttered off to sleep.
The old house rustles and the embers sigh.

It's hard to go to bed on such a night
And leave the fire talking to itself.
Forsake the tree, with all its colored light,
Abandon silver angels and lose sight
Of stockings hanging from the mantel shelf
And winter looking in, so blue and white.

Better to sit and watch the red coals glow
Within this room where love is everywhere,
Grown from a night two thousand years ago
When love was born among us here below,
When angels sang love in the shining air,
And shepherds sang it on the silver snow.

———

The Saturday Evening Post, December 23, 1950, p.62

My Neighbor John

My neighbor John, he was a patient one.
Worked hard, he did, and never did complain.
Up in the morning long before the sun,
Out in the field in cold or heat or rain,
Set in the ways of patience like a rock.
And John saved all the money he could earn
By farming steady as a ticking clock.
He knew someday his industry would turn
Into a golden harvest all his own,
And he could drop the handles of the plow,
And never turn a clod or lift a stone
Or stay up nights with a complaining cow,
Or break his back in damming up the creek.
And he was right. We buried him last week.

The Saturday Evening Post, October 2, 1948, p.79

Visiting

My house and father's house lie far apart,
And it's not often that we get to go
Visiting one another. Though the heart
Says "Go ahead," too many things say "No."

There's work to keep him home and keep me too.
And when the work is over, there's the weather.
Flood where he lives or blizzard where I do,
Or work and weather all mixed up together.

But when we do go visiting, it's fine
To rock before the fire, chair by chair,
And sip a cup of elderberry wine,
So close that I could touch him sitting there.

And somehow it's a task to go to bed.
A kind of nearness keeps us sitting up.
We rock and smile, and nothing much is said,
Each with a brimming heart and empty cup.

―――

The Saturday Evening Post, December 8, 1952, p.51

Swamp Turtle

More durable than calendar or clock,
A kinsman of the earth and child of ocean,
The snapping turtle, like a swimming rock,
Disturbs still water with deliberate motion.

His plate of armor, oddly chased and curled
And bound by gristle to a yellow base,
Slants upward through the dim green water world
Behind the pleated neck and wrinkled face,

Till first the lidded eye, as bright as blood,
And then the shell and claw emerge to climb
Out of the fundamental wet and mud
Grotesquely on a log to stare at time.

—————

The Saturday Evening Post, March 22, 1952, p.68

Stars and a Frog

Now down the old, star-stubbled field of night
Orion shoulders westward out of sight
And leaves a last few winter stars to lie
Like hobnails stamped upon the midnight sky.

But up the cloudy east new planets climb
The dark path leading them to summertime,
And far below where earth lies warm and wet
The first spring peeper plays his castanet.

———

The Saturday Evening Post, March 29, 1958, p.93

Wabash Catfish

Here where the muddy Wabash makes a slow
Curve between clay bank and grassy flat,
I'll sit awhile to watch the bubbles flow
And, Heaven willing, catch a yellow cat.

Below the river's coffee-colored skin
That ripples in the sun, old pussy feeds,
With whiskered antennae on his chin
To help him tell my worms from water weeds.

There! Have I hooked him now or hooked the world?
Or have I caught the boundary of a state?
No, here he comes, his heavy body curled
Against the strong, two-handed pull of fate.

Fate, did I say? Alas, the twisted thread
Snaps like a foolish hope, and down he shoulders,
With thrusting tail and wagging, bearded head
To sulk among drowned logs and bottom boulders.

―――

The Saturday Evening Post, July 21, 1956, p.77

Mr. Bumpy

Curious lump of living clay
With Gargoyle face and bleary eye,
Odd remnant of a distant day
When dragons ruled the earth and sky,
What do you think about, old toad?
What stirs within your ancient blood
While you hop down the dusty road
Or squat within the mossy wood?

Are you content with earthly holes
And hide that bears a wart or two,
Or do you envy orioles
Their wings that swing upon the blue?
Or would you rather be a frog,
A troubadour with yellow throat,
To chuckle love songs on a log
And wear a bottle-green dress coat?

The Saturday Evening Post, October 6, 1951, p.74

June Bug

The night is quiet. Distant and forlorn
The gentle voices of the city come.
Far off, the traffic blows a penny horn,
Motors are muted to an insect hum,
And tires murmur on another street
With whispered syllables and hushing noises.
The night goes tiptoeing on silent feet
But for these tired, drowsy little voices
That mutter in the dark and disappear.
So when the June bug strikes a savage blow
Against the screen, we startle up to hear
His anger bent against us like a bow,
The violence of his wings, the sudden jolt,
The impact like a tiny thunderbolt.

The Saturday Evening Post, June 30, 1951, p.79

Copperhead

Pick your path with wary foot.
Death lurks in the crooked root
And plays a grisly masquerade
With fallen limb and stippled shade.

His cheek is black, his eye is red,
He wears an ember for a head,
His tongue is like a fork of fire,
His tooth is sharper than desire.

Danger coiling, cold and thin,
Lightning in a mottled skin,
A dagger lifted for the blow,
An arrow strung on death's crossbow.

Better travel round about
Than enter in and not come out,
But if you venture, have a care—
Eternity is waiting there.

―――

The Saturday Evening Post, September 16, p.212

Closed Shop

The pond is full of frogs that come
Out upon the banks at night
With tuba, fife and kettledrum
To serenade the soft moonlight.

But if I venture down the hill,
The most innocuous of men,
They take my coming very ill
And plunge into the pool again.

This is a sorry thing to do
When I mean nothing but the best,
To help them sing a stave or two
As Vega sinks into the west.

The Saturday Evening Post, June 10, 1956, p.131

The Wayward Hen

Some wild impulse sent my hen
Cackling over the coop to go
Far from sight and sound of men
To lay an egg in this hedgerow.

Madness must have seized and shaken
Her poor wits out altogether,
To leave a snug henhouse forsaken
In this shrewd and nipping weather.

I'll not pick her up and take her,
Squawking and rebellious, back;
Such compulsion well might break her
Little brains to bric-a-brac.

Rather in this autumn thicket,
Squatting in her leafy pit
And clucking like a wildwood cricket,
She may set and she may sit.

———

The Saturday Evening Post, November 15, 1952, p.149

Starlight Abandoned

I went out to see the sun
Caged behind the bars of trees,
And hear the vespers, just begun,
Of meadow larks and chickadees,
To watch the whirlwind of the gnats,
Impalpable as spirits fled,
And stay until the wings of bats
Were hooked in darkness overhead.
No hurry, I had time to burn.
I meant to loaf and look my fill
And watch the wheel of starlight turn
Around the black hub of the hill.
Then came the cows out of the wood
And filed in slow sobriety
Across the pasture where I stood,
And halted there to wait for me.
They knew the path as well as I,
And I let down the pasture bars,
But there they stood beneath a sky
Already filling up with stars,
And there, of all their wits bereft,
Would stand eternally, I knew;
And so I led them home and left
Arcturus burning in the blue.

The Saturday Evening Post, May 28, 1949, p.147

Tin Roof

I climbed up on the barn this afternoon
With green paint brimming in a garden pail,
A black brush, wide and soft, a stirring spoon.
And hammer, too, for pounding any nail
That might have grown a half inch in the year
Gone into limbo since last I was here.
And like Stylites on his pinnacle,
I stared all afternoon and saw below
The rooting hogs, deep-voiced and cynical,
The ducks splay-footed in a quacking row,
The chickens mincing on their yellow toes,
The sleepy beagle in a dusty doze.
I took my time and found it time well spent
And saw the sun go down before I went.

―――

The Saturday Evening Post, June 18, 1949, p.67

Long Night

Because I couldn't sleep, I sat
Upon the porch till night wore thin,
Companioned by a neighbor's cat
Whose master wouldn't let him in.

He rubbed his ribs along my shin
And purred beneath a sable sky
Until we heard the birds begin
And morning opened up its eye.

———

The Saturday Evening Post, April 18, 1953, p.118

Long Legs

I love to watch a sand-hill crane
Knee-deep in pads and water flag,
Supported on his yellow cane
Like some sharp-shouldered feather bag
With bamboo legs and yard-long face,
Black-button eyes and crooked toes
That stiffly wade from place to place
While he looks down his endless nose.
As awkward as a bird can get,
A tripod with a pair of wings,
A hat rack come to life, and yet,
In flight the loveliest of things,
All angles beautifully aligned
With golden legs that trail behind.

The Saturday Evening Post, September 2, 1950, p.66

In the Garden

I find it hard to realize
That just an age or two ago
A dragon rolled his yellow eyes
Where now my red azaleas grow.

A pterodactyl spread his wings
And floated huge upon the skies
Where now a garden spider swings
Among the cabbage butterflies.

It would be interesting to know
What fate awaits my little plot
In half a billion years or so
When it is here and I am not.

The Saturday Evening Post, May 26, 1956, p.88

Morning Song

Today the wind is all about,
Cuffing the trees and puffing out
The pillowcases hung to dry.
The wind is all about the sky.

Today the sun is sweet and thin.
Open the shutters, let it in
To splash upon the rugs and pour
Golden puddles on the floor.

Today the robins, fat and proud,
Sound their tiny trumpets loud,
And all the pointed ears of spring
Are cocked to hear the robins sing.

―――――

The Saturday Evening Post, April 23, 1949, p.91

Crow

The hush of summer noon is deep,
The wheat is steeping in the sun,
The cows are lying half asleep
Down where the dry brook used to run.
Only the crow with bronchial wheeze
Clears his throat and coughs out loud,
Shivers in the sumac trees,
And hunching like a small black cloud
Wrapped in the nimbus of his wings,
Hoarsely damns the state of things.

———

The Saturday Evening Post, July 21, 1951, p.109

Tabby by Day—Tabby by Dark

When Tabby comes around to beg
A saucer of warm milk at noon,
She rubs her back against my leg
And purrs as loud as a bassoon,
Turns over and lifts helpless paws
As soft as velvet pads, and shows
Her petal tongue and hides her claws,
And pokes my hand with satin nose.

But I've seen her at midnight creep,
Hunting like a jungle cat,
Shadow-black and soft as sleep,
Sudden death for mouse or rat.
Tabby in the pale moonbeams,
Claws protruding from their sheath,
Eyes where cold green fire gleams,
And waiting jaws with needle teeth.

―――

The Saturday Evening Post, October 8, 1949, p. 121

Weather Vane

Here in this inland place where no
Seas resound or rivers flow,
We have an ocean made of air,
As deep as heaven and as fair,
As restless as the moving sea,
And bounded by eternity.

And high above all bottom things,
High on the courthouse tower swings
A lordly fish, all copper finned
And copper scaled, to tell the wind,
To stem the tide and swim the sea
That thunders over roof and tree.

―――

The Saturday Evening Post, January 22, 1949, p.114

Beech in the Wind

The stiff-backed beeches do not make
A bow to any sweeping wind,
But stand upright until they break.
Something within them will not bend!

I've seen them in the winter storms
Erect as pewter candlesticks,
Lifting up their branching arms
While spruce and poplar bend their necks.

An oak, with iron heart and hide
And branches muscled all their length,
Can well afford this sort of pride
And match the north wind, strength for strength.

But beeches have no right to stand
Intolerant of wind. They lie
Like shattered silver on the land
After the wind has trampled by.

———

The Saturday Evening Post, December 2, 1950, p.154

Train at Night

Somewhere a train spoke, low and lost and dim,
Remotely distant, far beyond the rim
Of silence that encircles this bright ground,
This winter field, constricted and frost bound.
There is no sound, there is no movement here,
The cold has laid a seal on tongue and ear,
Frozen the column of white smoke upright
Upon the roof to bear the weight of night,
And made the hollow, where a pond had been,
A mirror for the stars to gather in.
Then once again the train, disturbed and faint,
Breaks through the crust of quiet with complaint,
Comes closer, closer, gathers up its strength,
And shatters silence with its roaring length!

———

Good Housekeeping, December 1949, p.88

Thanksgiving Sonnet

Let us be thankful for unchanging things:
For green hills sleeping in a skin of grass,
For spring returning with a flash of wings,
For winter nights as clear as window glass
Set in a frame of sky for everyone
To see the silver stars. Let us remember
Gladly the great promise of the sun,
That walks a golden road in gray November
And scatters brightness everywhere to show,
Though winter comes, it will not last always.
Let us rejoice in all the good we know
That flows forever through our nights and days,
Stemming its steady way from God above—
A river broad as faith and deep as love.

The Saturday Evening Post, November 27, 1948, p.140

Imprisoned Spring

The endless rows of office buildings rise
To lock the balmy twilight up in bars
Of reinforced concrete. I lift my eyes
And, far above me, see escaping stars
Slipping to westward over cliffs of stone.
Black shadows lie like furrows on the walk,
And out of them a yellow flower has grown—
A street light like a jonquil on a stalk
Of hollow iron, green as if it were
A living country stem, which it is not.
I miss the touch of pussy-willow fur,
The choir of robins and the garden plot,
And, if I could, I'd trade LaSalle Street now
For forty acres and a bull-tongue plow.

The Saturday Evening Post

Cicada

When summer stamps a golden hoof
And leaps the mountain of the sky,
I clamber up a hilltop's roof
And cheer him on with strident cry.

No great accomplishment, I know,
And not a lofty height, it's true,
But that's as far as I can go,
And that's as much as I can do.

If I were gifted like a bird
With music and the mighty wings,
Why then, perhaps, you would have heard
Me singing where the skylark sings.

But even as it is, I'll hum
As loud as any bumblebee
And pound my little kettledrum
Till winter puts a stop to me.

The Saturday Evening Post

Brown Winter

We have no place to water stock.
The brook's a sunken spine of rock,
The pond a socket, brown and dry
And empty of its azure eye,
The spring a web of weed and dust,
The well itself a broken trust.

I dare not strike a match outside.
The grass is drought-and-winter dried,
And every twig or crooked stick
Or milkweed pod a withered wick,
And every leaf a dry desire
To cup a golden grain of fire.

―――

The Saturday Evening Post, January 2, 1954, p.61

Time Song

Time, old enemy, you tramp in vain
Upon these sodded hills and waves of grass.
They sink beneath your feet and lift again,
Indifferent to the scythe and hourglass.
The lusty earth, the valley's curling clover,
The ridge's muscled back, the greening plain,
The pelt of grass that covers old scars over—
All these grow young beneath the sun and rain.
Go rob the blossom from a baby's skin,
Or drift your snow into an old man's hair;
Wither the fat until their shanks are thin,
And cast your net of wrinkles on the fair.
But leave the earth alone and heaven, too,
And lovers' hearts, for these make light of you.

The Saturday Evening Post, March 29, 1952, p.94

View Shift

There have been moments when I thought
Joy was a singing bird I'd caught
And when I felt that I could hold
Life in my hands like miser's gold.
I walked upon a summer world,
Beneath my feet the flowers curled,
Around my head the robins flew,
And time was a laughing boy I knew.

But cool, quicksilver robin notes
Cease with the throbbing of their throats,
The snow will sift white petals down,
The tender leaf turn brittle brown.
My heart, put not your dearest trust
In youth or years, for they do rust
Like iron down to nothingness,
But trust in love and nothing less.

The Saturday Evening Post, October 25, 1952, p.146

Fire Fall

Something jars the sky to send
Stars tumbling down, end over end,
Catching fire and leaving trails
Behind them like red swallowtails,
Till they're no longer stars at all
But only cinders left to fall,
And then a little ash, I guess,
And finally only nothingness.
Now I can sort out fact and fiction
And blame this holocaust on friction,
But what the something is that jars
The autumn night and shakes the stars
Like apples off a tree…well, I
Have never found out what or why.

The Saturday Evening Post, October, 1960

Summer Sleep

The brook dried up, and trees along the lane
Were coated white with dust.
The jay bird cried and cried
Each afternoon to call a rain
That never came, and the whole countryside
Slumbered together underneath the sun.
With head between his paws, the spotted hound
Whined in a dream, and in the chicken run
Hens slept in feathered bundles on the ground
Only the lizard scuttled in the heat,
His eyes alert and curious and bright.
The green tail following the tiny feet
Into a cord of wood and out of sight,
While overhead the summer, fast asleep,
Lay quiet as a pond, but ocean-deep.

The Saturday Evening Post, August 7, 1948, p.116

Sunrise on Wheels

When I got up today, I found
Rain still hammering the ground,
Fog in plenty, east wind, too,
All the sky bruised black and blue,
And now and then a blast of thunder
Loud enough to make me wonder
If the world would last the day
Or if some prop had given way.

Then rising through the mist and chill,
The school bus clattered up our hill,
And peering out, I thought I spied
All tomorrow packed inside
Like seeds within a curious pod,
Mechanized and rubber-shod,
And though it passed me by, I knew
We'd have another day or two.

The Saturday Evening Post, May 26, 1951, p.56

Fire by Night

I guess Luke never rightly knew
From what red seed the fire grew,
But red roots ran across the floor,
Blood-red petals climbed the door,
Burning runners leaped the gable,
Blossomed red in barn and stable,
And shook off the scarlet bees to swarm
The bright red flower of a farm.

Luke, he never said a word,
But stood there like some awkward bird,
Beyond the roaring rim of light
That bound the crater in the night,
And watched the fire flower die
Bit by bit out of the sky,
Till all grew dark again and dim,
And blackness entered into him.

The Saturday Evening Post, April 19, 1952, p.203

The Night Watch

Last night as I lay wrapped in quiet dark,
A neighbor's dog, with sudden, senseless bark
Shattered my dream; then growled himself to sleep,
While silence settled down again bone-deep.
But there all broad-awake upon my bed,
My eyes somehow propped open in my head,
The very stillness buzzing in my ears,
I wooed oblivion for a hundred years.
I heard the candle of the moon go out
And listened to a star that groped about
Somewhere between my chimney and the sky,
And once I heard a wind wake up and sigh,
And then doze off, until at last the sun
Exploded like a bomb, and night was done.

―――

The Saturday Evening Post, June 25, 1855, p.129

Caleb and the Frogs

Old Caleb McCann was the kind of man
Who jogs along the best he can
And gives nobody no trouble, except
Maybe his wife. His wife, she kept
Caleb pretty well under her thumb.
She said that Caleb, he troubled her some.
And sure, he tippled a little bit. Who
Wouldn't, with her to come home to?
Then late one night, on his way from town,
Caleb got lost and wandered down
The bottom land to the cranberry bogs,
With no one to tell him the path but frogs.
The little frogs out in the swamp; they said
"Cut-across, cut-across, come right ahead!"
But the big bullfrog with a hollow sound
Sang, "Caleb-go-round! Caleb-go-round!"
And his wife, she waited all night and day,
But Caleb, he never came back that way.
And if you should ask me how he did go,
I couldn't tell, but the frogs—they know.

The Saturday Evening Post, December 4, 1948, p.70

Stray Pine

How it came there, I don't know.
No reason for a pine to grow
Deep in the middle of a maple wood.
Eighty feet high the maples stood,
Strong of limb and stout of root,
With one small pine tree underfoot,
Crowded up and shut in there
By legs of maples everywhere.

A thing like that would bother me,
I'd rather be a maple tree
If all the others were. But it
Didn't seem to mind a bit,
Got along with the maples fine,
Just went right on being a pine,
And they didn't seem to care about it.
Gospel truth—but you may doubt it.

―――

The Saturday Evening Post, October 23, 1948, p.114

Objection

Only a month or two gone by
We sat outdoors and watched the moon
Squat like a pumpkin in the sky
And heard a locust scratch a tune.
And I for one resent the blight
That's settled since on field and tree;
I'd like to know what legal right
A winter's got to fall on me.
Why should a blizzard bare its teeth
To nip my fingers and my feet
Or bury all my walks beneath
A ton or two of frozen sleet?
If I could serve a writ, in short,
I'd take the season straight to court.

The Saturday Evening Post, January 1, 1955, p.44

Salamander

Complain about it if you will.
Sweat and stifle, speak of snow,
Long for winter and the chill
Crawl of flesh when blizzards blow.
Conjure up December storm,
Dream of frozen pond and river;
If you feel July too warm,
Clasp a cake of ice and shiver,
But beneath the sun I lie,
Freckling myself all over,
Happy as a bird in sky,
Fish in water, cow in clover,
And you shall not wring from me
One small tear of sympathy.

―――――

The Saturday Evening Post

Sun

And now the lion of July,
With yellow mane and burning eye,
Has risen in the east to tread
The empty desert of the sky.

Before him all the clouds are fled,
Behind him all the winds are dead,
And where he passes, flowers die
And wheat bows down its heavy head.

―――――

The Saturday Evening Post, July 2, 1949, p.88

Going Back

I felt like Gulliver in Lilliput
When I went back there after all this time.
The place was just as I remembered, but
Diminished from a dollar to a dime.
I reached and picked an apple from the bough
Of that tall tree we were afraid to climb.
The big old belfry tower's tiny now,
And tinkles when the bells begin to chime.
Do you recall the giant who lived within
That corner house we had to pass each day?
I hardly knew him, he had grown so thin,
And his poor dog had dwindled quite away.
But when I met our old school-teacher, then
It was my turn to shrink boy-size again.

The Saturday Evening Post, September 18, 1948, p.147

Sun in the Morning

Before the sun, I climbed up Turkey Hill,
Leaving my footprints in the frosty stubble
And night behind me in the valley still.
I climbed from smoky rooms and talk and trouble
And all the jigsaw handiwork of man
To where I walked upon a limestone floor
Laid down by angels when the world began,
Roofed over by the sky and walled with four
Great cliffs of sky and windowed by the sky.
And there I watched the flower of new day
Blossom upon the east and fill the eye
With glory and with faith. I turned away
At last to walk reluctant back toward night,
And saw instead the valley paved with light.

The Saturday Evening Post, October 16, 1948, p.171

Subway Soliloquy

When I get money enough, I'll buy
A scrap of land and a snip of sky,
With maybe a creek to set it off
And serve a bird for a drinking trough,
And a tree to shelter a tiny house
Where I'll live, calm as a country mouse.

I'll be there, if you care to look,
Slumbering by the sleepy brook,
Or marrying bulbs to a bit of earth,
Or reckoning up a rainbow's worth,
Or strolling the boundary, soft and slow,
Listening to my whiskers grow.

———

The Saturday Evening Post, August 14, 1954, p.75

Cleaning Lady

Tuesday morning much too soon,
Just as sun supplants the moon,
Mrs. Klopf arrives to start
Taking all the house apart.

Thick and wide as she is long,
Mrs. Klopf is very strong,
And with bucket, mop and broom
Fights and conquers every room.

Cobwebs fall before her wrath,
Children scuttle from her path,
Dogs and cats and mice together
Run out into zero weather.

But on Wednesday, ah, the calm
Settles down like healing balm;
Dogs and cats and mice and men
And cobwebs venture back again.

―――

The Saturday Evening Post, December 14, 1954, p.48

The Winter Harbor

It seemed a fearful place to me,
A mountain scarred by a plunging street
That fell from a tipple to a sea
Gray as sorrow and cold as sleet.

What could it be but a port of death,
With black ships moored to a frozen dock
And ever the sea with foggy breath
And jaws of ice at the ribs of rock?

But then along the rim of land
Beside the wharves and iron hulls
Came little children, hand in hand,
To play like flocks of piping gulls.

And all along the water's lips
Their laughter rose up like a fountain
Till lights sprang out upon the ships
And windows shone upon the mountain.

Ladies' Home Journal, February 1956, p.155

My Urban Aunt

Where tentacles of smoke embrace the sky
And trucks make noises and a siren wails
My aunt lives in a small apartment by
The trains that thunder past on ringing rails.
The walls in Auntie's house are very thin,
The neighbors shout all day and show no pity,
And every night she has to sleep within
A kind of drum that's pounded by the city.
And yet do you suppose she gives a care?
Is it your thought that Auntie minds a bit?
Would she, you feel, be happier elsewhere,
Despite her years of getting used to it?
Why sure, she hates the place and gladly would
Exchange it for Tahiti, if she could.

The Saturday Evening Post, March 11, 1961, p.102

Miss Mattie

As long as Miss Mattie's front steps are clean,
The earth could turn blue and the heavens green;
I see her each day darting out of her room
To whirl like a dervish with bucket and broom.
Her spectacles jig on the end of her nose,
And the morning is filled with her flying elbows.
And when in the winter the innocent snow
Covers the wrinkled old city below,
She straddles a step with a cloud on her brow
And scatters the snow like a rotary plow.
Miss Mattie, I pray that the merciful Lord
May grant you this wish for a lasting reward:
Not wings or a harp or a place in the choir,
But a golden broom and your heart's desire,
To sweep all the stars in the Milky Way
Down all the golden stairs each day.

———

The Saturday Evening Post, May 22, 1948, p.108

Allegheny Front

Blue with shade and tawny with sun,
These mountains lie upon green meadows.
Patched and mottled black and dun,
They move and breathe with sun and shadows.

At night they shoulder out the stars,
And mist of indigo climbs creeping
Through the black and silver bars,
Caged in moonlight—lions sleeping.

―――

Poetry Chap Book, Winter 1944-45

River Worry

What puzzles me whenever I think on it
Is how a man can grow a hill of beans
Up here, the way the river carries down it
Enough good mud to bury New Orleans.
You'd think one spring would strip us to the bone
And leave us sitting on a limestone ridge,
With every furrow in the garden gone
Hell bent for Natchez underneath the bridge.
Just take a look out there and see the river
Boiling along, a half a mile of flood,
And then sit back and figure that forever
Is one long time to keep on losing mud.
And tell me, if you can, how long I've got
Before New Orleans gets my whole bean plot.

———

The Saturday Evening Post, May 15, 1948, p.146

Old Riddle

There is a kind of blindness that comes over
The eyes that look upon a child or lover,
Or upon anyone beloved and dear.
Men see no error there, nor error hear,
But see instead a shining grace, apart
From other matters. They look with the heart
And listen with their love, and all they know
Is visible and heard, and hence is so.
I have seen flowers rising from the sand,
And leaves uncurling green from barren land,
And rainbows out of storm, and I have heard
Beauty come singing from a crippled bird,
And watched love look at love, until I feel
Theirs is the vision and my blindness real.

———

Good Housekeeping, 1948

The Planting

They touched the field with fire, and the wind
Gathered the red tongues up into the air.
The warm rain fell, the sunlight waited there
Upon black soil and stubble, fire-thinned.
Then on a frosty morning when the team
Stamps and strains against the plow's bright knife,
The field is wakened once again to life,
The earth is opened and the furrows steam.
Sun warms a cradle for the new-born things,
Resting his yellow hands upon the clods,
And now the men sow the living seed like gods,
With crows to watch them, leaning on their wings
Above the dark earth all the golden day.
Again the angel rolls the stone away.

———

The Saturday Evening Post, March 27, 1948

Magic

Long overdue, spring kept us waiting here
With winter weather deep into the year.
Bare trees, bare ground and winter sky swept bare
Of birds or clouds—white, barren, dry and clear,
With wind to pinch the fingers black and blue
And send smoke gusting down the chimney flue.
And cold as iron, day succeeded day,
Cold as the metal runners of a sleigh.
Until the sun, abruptly, without warning,
Caught like a fire in an April morning,
Licked up the heaven in a scarlet flame,
Routed the winter; and the springtime came
Easy as breath, with orchard petals blowing,
New green leaves, and brimming gutters flowing.

―――――

The Saturday Evening Post, April 10, 1948, p.70

Winter Memory

A half a mile of valley huddles down
Until December. Fields are barren brown
With stubble and dry leaves and broken stalk.
On empty branches only jay birds talk,
And overhead the sky hangs heavy gray.
It takes a clock to tell the time of day,
It takes a calendar to make a man
Remember spring, believe it if he can;
And in the stove it takes a lot of wood
To stir up summer in the winter blood
And make a memory of sun at noon
Burning a red hole down, or of the moon,
Yellow and low, with katydids all squeaking,
Or the heavy voice of thunder speaking.

―――

The Saturday Evening Post, December 20, 1947

Kite Time

Skipper, put up that dusty book and come
Outside into the roaring, sunny weather.
You hear that March wind beating like a drum?
You see that red kite pulling on a tether?
Look up, son, all the air is full of motion,
The swaying, dipping, swooping, reeling kites.
They bob like colored corks on a blue ocean.
They plunge like meteors in erratic flights.
They buck and rear and paw the windy sky.
They toss and dart and leap straight up for joy.
Purple, crimson, yellow, green they fly,
And every one held by a grinning boy.
So come on, skipper, come on outside and
Try holding shooting stars in your small hand.

―――

The Saturday Evening Post, March 13, 1948

Lake People

The Cottagers

The cottagers descend like locusts from
South Bend, Fort Wayne, Columbus, Kokomo,
By car, by bike, by bus, by train, and some
Hitch-hiking from Terre Haute or Chicago.
Like locusts, winter finds them buried in
Dark shelters, dormant melancholy pupae
Like locusts, summer finds them shedding skin
Along the lake, as naked as a kewpie.
Snakes and flies and cottagers in May
Hatch out and cluster thick as swarming bees.
Warm-weather visitors, they seldom stay
Beyond the goldenrod. The first thin freeze
That crackles on the lake like cellophane
Drives them away by car, by bus, by train.

———

Prairie Schooner, Spring 1945

Lake People

Ditch Diggers

Crow Beach is low land merging into lake,
Green meadows coming down to meet the bay.
A row of cottages without a break
For half-a-mile. The little children play
Along the shallows there. The mothers know
It's safe enough. With buckets in their hands
And pants rolled up, the little children go
Along the water's lips to dig the sands
This is a business for the young and grave,
To dig a ditch and keep the water out,
To see it flooded by a reaching wave
And crumble in and vanish while you shout.
To hollow out another and another.
And dig and dig until it's time for mother.

———

Prairie Schooner, Spring 1945

Lake People
Chris Swenson

Chris Swenson lives on Cedar Point and owns
An old piano and three racing scows.
There is a wall of weedy cobblestones
That hooks out in the lake, and Chris allows
No better harbor, good for anything
From sheltering mosquitoes and stray cows
To snakes in summer, spawning pike in spring,
Pond lilies, white and gold, and sunken boughs,
And frogs that sit around the edge and sing
A bass accompaniment to curious tunes
Played on the black keys in the summer night,
Chris conjuring the ghosts of ancient runes,
Outside three sailboats, glimmering and white,
And music walking on the dark lagoons.

Prairie Schooner, Spring 1945

Lake People

Elvira Ball

Farmer Ball came quite awhile before
The landlords with their stucco and white paint
And matchstick cottages with one screen door.
Elvira shifts his chew and says he ain't
Prepared to trade his barn for one. It stands
Upright and silver gray along the shore.
A hundred years ago, with his own hands,
Great-grandpa built a barn. That long and more.
When all of this is gone, that barn will be
As sound and solid as a horse's hoof,
Sheltering mice and cats and timothy,
With hickory shingles curled up on the roof.
The barn will be there, says Elvira; you
Will likely be dead, but I'll be here too.

Prairie Schooner, Spring 1945

Lake People

Sarah Ball

When Sarah Ball, Elvira's wife, was young
She was baptized in winter. That was years
Ago, of course, and while the hymns were sung
She stood in water shivering to her ears.
Elvira saw her there in Buttons Bay,
Her white skirts floating, and his heart appears
To have been forfeit to her right away.
He swears that she wept icicles for tears,
And says he knew as soon as ever he saw
Her able to stand that—she could stand him.
He says it took her fourteen days to thaw,
And on the fifteenth, to a marriage hymn,
She became Mrs. Ball. Elvira told
Me proudly that she never caught a cold.

―――

Prairie Schooner, Spring 1945

Lake People

Tim Bacon

Tim Bacon must have seen the glaciers tear
The top soil from this lake bed long ago.
I'm sure he's old enough to have been there,
And from his knowledge of the lake, it must be so.
Tim knows the hole where standard bluegills go
To hover cool on summer afternoons;
When winds are right and water indigo,
He trolls for green pike with his silver spoons.
See yonder, Tim says, by that sunken dredge,
A few perch weeds, and water brown as tea?
Well, ten feet underneath there is a ledge.
Come morning, that's where bass are apt to be.
I'll tell you what. I'll stop for you at four.
Will you be up? I'll knock at the side door.

Prairie Schooner, Spring 1945

Lake People

Doc Preston

Doc Preston drove his Ford right through the ice
In January. He was making time
Across the lake to help Cornelia Price
Have twins. I wouldn't wager a thin dime
On anybody's chances there in winter
Twenty feet down, but Doc climbed out the door,
Twenty feet down, I said, and in ice water.
Swam out somehow. He got there just before
The twins. Cornelia was in one twin bed;
They had to put Doc Preston in the other.
Those twins know who their daddy is, he said,
But damned if they'll know which one is their mother.
What happened to the Ford? Well, late in May
They pulled it out. It's parked across the way.

Prairie Schooner, Spring 1945

Lake People

Old Gettels

He anchors in about ten feet and baits
Five cane poles. They stick out like spiders'
Legs around the boat. Old Gettels waits,
Humped up and patient, for bluegills and shiners.
He waits, too, in the same slow stolid fashion
For God's wrath, sure someday to break upon us
About election time, to purge the nation.
Old Gettels always votes for Norman Thomas.
Under the round straw hat, his blue eyes, sharp
To pin stupidity, peer at five bobbers,
And thoughts of perch, Republicans, and carp
Are mixed with pike and Democrats and robbers.
For bass Old Gettels likes a chub or cricket,
But for himself, he'll take the left wing ticket.

Prairie Schooner, Spring 1945

Lake People

Empido's Swamp

In back of Johnson's Bay the railroad runs
Two rusty tracks across Empido's swamp.
Here, between trains, the snapping turtle suns
Himself on muck hills, and the beavers camp
In tents of mud and straw. Great, clumsy cranes
Build black nests in the branches of drowned trees.
A thick canal winds through the swamp and drains
Sluggish and green and choked with jointed reeds,
Into the sparkling waters of the bay.
Some time ago old man Empido said
He'd fill the swamp. He thought that it would pay
To put up cottages, but he's been dead
A good while now. They searched it more or less
But had no luck. He's out there yet, I guess.

Prairie Schooner, Spring 1945

Morning on Windy Hill

When all the valley still is quenched in night,
The morning catches fire on Windy Hill
And spreads all down the eastern slope until
The whole high pasture there is burning bright.

Then with each cloud that drifts across the sun,
And with each wind that walks upon the grass,
The shifting colors of the meadow pass
From green to golden, from golden into dun.

And rolling acres of the sky lean down
So close above the field, a man could stand
Upright, with both his feet set firm on land,
And wear the clear blue heaven for a crown.

―――――

The Saturday Evening Post, October 1, 1949, p.114

Donnegan's Notion

My friend, old Donnegan, he has a notion
That once these hills were waves upon the sea,
And all these ridges rolled upon an ocean.
"Any old fool can tell that much," says he.
"Look at the lay of them, they're waves, all right,
Stopped in a storm when God held up his hand.
Just when the north wind blew with all its might,
And sea reached skyward, sudden all was land.
It's clear enough to me," he says. "What's more,
I've plowed up sea shells in a field of hay
And seen the gravel of an old seashore
Beneath this clover patch. 'Most any day,
Unless we mend our ways, and maybe then,
I say these ridges might turn to waves again."

———

The Saturday Evening Post, September 3, 1949, p.64

Wasps

I don't see how in thunder they get in!
The screens are new this year, and tight as skin.
And yet, somehow, whenever noonday comes,
Here are the wasps by dozens, hopping mad,
Beating against the screen until it drums,
Trying to get back out, I wish we had
A one-way hole that let them out to stay.
Why did the good Lord make wasps anyway?

―――

The Saturday Evening Post, July 30, 1949, p.91

Scarecrow

A scarecrow ought to frighten things away
And flap his rags at hawk and crow and jay,
But I believe each pest upon the farm
Finds welcome here beneath your tattered arm.
The field mice entertain their kin and kith
Inside the good wheat straw we stuffed you with,
And every sunup finds your waistline thinner
From furnishing their relatives a dinner.

See here, this curling morning-glory vine
Has spiraled up around your hickory spine,
And from the way your hat is pecked and pried,
A blackbird must be keeping house inside.
Look how round-shouldered this old coat has grown
From fat crows roosting on your collarbone,
And if I didn't like your merry face,
I'd put a meaner scarecrow in your place.

The Saturday Evening Post, July 23, 1949, p.60

Back Country

These ridges wrinkle up the earth and hold
A scattering of men in every fold—
Men pretty much cut off from everything,
With drifts in winter, mud hub-deep in spring,
Crops to be kept in summer, and in fall
No better hunting anywhere at all
Than right at home. Why bother to come out?
Who cares what other people are about?
We have the solid earth beneath our feet,
Our hill of sugar corn, our patch of wheat,
And every spring our furrows for the seed,
And every fall our crops and cattle feed,
And, after seventy years the Lord has given,
A chance to plant ourselves and grow in heaven.

The Saturday Evening Pot, May 14, 1949, p.49

Fawn

He must have seen me sitting there,
Square on the stump. He must have seen.
But whether or no, he didn't care,
But stepped through willows budded green
And sniffed a taste of April air,
For all the world as if I'd been
A thousand miles from anywhere,
And not right under his velvet chin.
I sat quiet as I could sit,
And thought as quiet as I could think.
Then, sudden, he was aware of it,
And bolted before I could even blink.
And all I saw of him from then on
Was a wink of brown and a white tail gone.

The Saturday Evening Post, April 9, 1949, p.167

Mouse

Deep in the night, when you and all
The two-legged noises are quiet in bed,
The mouse comes out of the pantry wall,
First his whiskers and then his head,
Then his tiny front feet; and there
He stops for a minute to look before
Venturing out in the open where
A terrible cat might tread the floor.

His little eyes shine like drops of ink.
His ears are cocked for a hint of sound,
He twitches his nose, and quick as a wink
And soft as a shadow that leaps on the ground,
He races a dozen feet after a crumb,
Swallows it down with a will, and then,
Fast as a finger can snap on a thumb,
Scurries back home to his hole again.

―――

The Saturday Evening Post, February 26, 1949, p.124

New Day

Some January mornings ring as bright
As if a bell had risen with the sun.
The music of the morning routs the night,
And peals of light come singing down upon
An iron earth, a river hard as stone,
A distant hill brought magically near,
A world resounding with the golden tone
Of morning bringing in a brand-new year,
And yet as quiet as the smoke that ties
White ribbons from the chimneys to the skies.

―――

The Saturday Evening Post, January 1, 1949, p.40

The Gifts

He acts as if each day were given him
For Christmas, just as eager, just as proud,
With dawn arriving and the starlight dim
And sunrise flooding up a crimson cloud.
And there the morning, waiting for his hand
To break the cord of night and unwrap day
And scatter it broadcast upon the land.
He turns to me and smiles as if to say,
"Well now, have you ever seen the like?"
Or when a tree leafs out or thrushes sing,
Or when he see a bolt of lightning strike,
It's all brand new. There's not a blessed thing
He ever gets used to, and some folks hold
He acts too childish for a man grown old.

———

The Saturday Evening Post, December 18, 1948, p.101

Giant Sleeping

The river holds the land in heavy arms.
Sprawled out in slumber, lazily it twists
A thick brown body over valley farms,
With bridges manacled upon its wrists
And levees jacketing the muddy flesh.
By dam and cable belted round, it lies,
A giant sleeping in the netted mesh
Of cords as strong as pygmies can devise.

The Saturday Evening Post, November 6, 1948, p.165

Wind and Fire

I've never known a night so cold before,
With rivers locked and bolted into place,
And north wind swaggering the valley floor
To shake the very house upon its base.
I hear him now, a hollow, booming roar
That makes a cannon of the chimney stack.
He hammers at the latch and kicks the door,
Then reels away to fetch the barn a crack.
But here I sit, almost upon the blaze
Of crackling hickory logs. With drowsy eyes
I stare into the fire and see a maze
Of scarlet flowers, flaming August skies,
And embers like a sun. Why should I fear
What winter does, with summer burning here?

The Saturday Evening Post, January 28, 1956, p.105

Easter Parade

Easter sun looks down and blesses
Little girls in pastel dresses,
Ruffled at the hems and sleeves
And prettier than budding leaves.

Curiously void of noise
March the brand-new suited boys,
Slicked and burnished and subdued,
Currycombed and Sunday-shoed.

Just behind each little flock
Two resplendent parents walk,
While the bells in every steeple
Call to all the shining people.

The Saturday Evening Post, April 9, 1955, p.104

Sundown

Of horizontal light, of long blue shade,
Of children singing is the evening made.
Of sunshine gathered in lace curtains barred
With shadows of the frame, and in the yard
Brown earth gilt over with a tawny crust,
And in the air bright particles of dust.

Of this is evening made, and of the dark
That rises from the ground and climbs the bark
Up shaggy hickories to quench the light
Flaming in leaves above the lifting night.
And always children singing home from play,
Golden in the sun's last level ray.

Ladies' Home Journal, March 1955, p.113

Witch Trouble

If rats grow fat and pigs grow thin
And cows keep night awake with mooing,
Witches must be getting in.
This kind of thing is all their doing.

Go paint the barn with witch windows
And make a cross your weathervane.
Hang horseshoes up and plant hedgerows
Of Judas tree and witch's bane.

Be courteous to cats and keep
A rabbit's foot or four-leaf clover
Under the pillow when you sleep,
And say your prayers twice over.

———

The Saturday Evening Post, February 3, 1951, p.78

Midwinter

Now all the days are gray and white,
And all alike and briefly done,
Each with a single rose of light
That flowers in the setting sun.

The sky is drifted deep in snow,
The sun is like a silver moon,
And only the gray shadows know
White morning from white afternoon.

———

The Saturday Evening Post, January 20, 1951, p.76

White Magic

Here is a magic made last night—
A pasture polished diamond bright,
A frog pond sealed in cellophane,
A frost web on a windowpane,
An oak tree in a glassy skin,
A pump with bearded mouth and chin,
And all the meadows wrapped in snow,
Tied with a brook in a silver bow.

The Saturday Evening Post, January 6, 1951, p.61

Abigail

Abagail, Abagail, how can you sit
Hour upon hour to knit and to knit,
Season by season and weather by weather
Clicking and clacking your needles together,
Ticking and tocking as dull as a clock,
Dimming your eyes over sweater and sock?

Thunder may bellow and set the roof rocking;
You keep on turning the heel of a stocking.
Robbers might leave me for dead in a ditch;
You'd take the news without dropping a stitch,
And even if Bessie, the cow, had a kitten,
You would keep knitting the thumb of a mitten.

Abigail, Abigail, hearken to time
Pattering by like the beat of a rhyme.
Life is a dower that mustn't be wasted,
Love is a cordial that ought to be tasted,
And lips like a flower can surely do better
Than counting the stitches in sock or in sweater.

———

The Saturday Evening Post, November 11, 1950, p.112

November Song

I have seen death all autumn long
Twisting the blood-red leaves away,
Stripping the branches of bird song,
And webbing all the world in gray.
And now the stubbled acres lie
About me barren as a stone,
And ice has gathered in the sky
To bleach the valley white as bone.

Thanks be to God for what we know,
That death is but another birth.
The living soil beneath the snow,
The sleeping seed within the earth,
The passion of the sun in spring
Will lift green life out of the clay
And harry death on dusky wing
Before the golden light of day.

―――

The Saturday Evening Post, November 4, 1950, p.165

Autumn Protest

These gaudy copper rags and sparkling shreds
Of golden finery suit a gypsy queen,
But why should trees insist on yellow heads
And spangled skirts instead of decent green?
Behold the sumac like a painted clown,
The maples that a rainbow must have kissed,
Grandmother oaks that should have settled down,
All wearing ruby clusters on each wrist.
And even the prim orchard reeling drunk
With apples wrapped in lemon-colored leaves,
Bright amber gum that oozes on the trunk,
Fat pears and shining plums, and all for thieves
That hide with dripping beak inside the trees
And share the sticky sweet with honeybees.

―――――

The Saturday Evening Post, September 30, 1950, p. 47

Mare Apparent

Looks like ten acres ought to keep
A mare content. The grass grows deep,
The water hole brims fresh and blue,
And there's her colt for company, too.
But let the board fence spring a chink,
And out she squirms to steal a drink
At our rain barrel or lie at ease
On cabbage patch or plot of peas.

I find her rolling on her back
Between the well house and wood shack,
Or nipping yellow daisy heads,
Or sampling petunia beds,
Or hiding with a purple chin
Arbor-deep in grapes and sin,
Or standing where the orchard dapples
Shade upon her, eating apples.

The Saturday Evening Post, August 26, 1950, p.112

Drought

Arms of lightning shake the sky,
Thunderheads are mountain high,
Blotting all the stars that show
And blackening the earth below.
Hear the sullen summer thunder
Threatening to roll us under,
Warning us with kettledrums
Of a rain that never comes.
Morning will be clear as glass,
Noon a shining bowl of brass,
Sunset stained a bloody red,
Night another thunderhead,
And day by day a thirsty hand
Will tighten on this dusty land.

―――

The Saturday Evening Post, July 29, 1950, p.80

After the Ball

Do you remember coming home that night?
How very late it was and clear and still?
And how the stars hung low and clustered tight
Together like a crown upon the hill?
And when the headlights turned and swept the lawn,
Do you remember what it was we found?
The rabbits dancing there before the dawn
On nimble velvet feet on velvet ground.
You laughed at my surprise and said they had
A way of dancing to a lilting tune
Unheard by us. And come good days or bad,
Each summer night, you said, beneath the moon
They dance for joy and shall, long after we
Have danced our last and paid the fiddler's fee.

The Saturday Evening Post, June 24, 1950, p.104

Buzzard

The turkey buzzard circles round
And rarely moves a wing to fly
And seldom settles on the ground,
But draws his arc upon the sky
With slow, exact geometry,
As if he were exempted from
Old Newton's law of gravity.
As steady as a pendulum,
Deliberate as a second hand,
Inevitable as the night,
Around and round above the land,
He circles like death's satellite
And marks the living flesh and bone
As ultimately for his own.

The Saturday Evening Post, April 29, 1950, p.132

Rainy Easter

April, April, hear me pray:
Lift this curse of smoky gray
Wrapped and tied upon the world,
Keeping soul and body curled
In a cramped cocoon of fog,
Fit for only newt or frog.

April, April, let there be
Sunlight strung on every tree,
Tulips flaming up like fire,
Robins shouting in a choir,
And rainbows laughing in a sky
Bluer than a baby's eye.

───

The Saturday Evening Post, April 8, 1950, p.142

Storm Cellar

Deep in the shadowy cellar where
The furnace lifted up its arms,
My grandpa kept a rocking chair,
And when the first far-off alarms
Of coming thunder squalls were heard,
When lightning lit my grandma's eye
And crackled in her every word,
And clouds of wrath were drawing nigh,
My grandpa would clomp down the stair
And, with the furnace door ajar,
Would sit and rock and fill the air
With tranquil smoke from his cigar,
Until he judged that time and love
Had scattered all the storms above.

The Saturday Evening Post, March 25, 1950, p.150

February Sun

This golden bumper of a day should be
Sent back and bottled up. It has no right
To sparkle here and dazzle you and me
Until our eyes have tippled up its light
And swear they see bright summer everywhere,
Painting the sky with morning-glory blue,
Piping a love song in the melting air,
And beading stubble fields with silver dew.
Take my advice and keep indoors today,
Pull down the shades and push away the sun.
One taste of springtime doesn't make a May,
More snow is sure to fall when day is done.
And if you take this counterfeit for gold,
You'll find the rest of winter twice as cold.

The Saturday Evening Post, February 11, 1950, p.125

Mending Days

On a day like this when the wind breaks loose,
And the sky is feathered as gray as a goose,
And the snow so deep it makes you fear
Spring might never get back this year,
Then is a time to darn a sock,
Or mend the hand of a broken clock,
Or cure a chair with a case of shakes,
Or fix the kitchen pump. It takes
A day like this for mending things,
When winter spreads its gray goose wings.

The Saturday Evening Post, January 21, 1950, p.43

North Wind

Over the frozen courthouse clock
And iron streets and ponds of glass
And gardens bare and hard as rock,
And over the bones of leaves and grass,
The North Wind howls a banshee song
And cracks a whip of cutting sleet,
Scourges earth with a knotted thong,
And wraps it white in a winding sheet.

―――

The Saturday Evening Post, December 3, 1949, p.109

Winter Weary

I am heartsick of armor-bound
Acres fixed in iron frost,
Bones of trees in frozen ground,
Barked in sleet and winter-tossed.

Sick of fields where winter walks
And where the ghost-white rabbit runs
Between the bent and hollow stalks
Of summer's rooted skeletons.

Winter-weary as a crow
I stand upon wind-scoured ice
And watch eternal snowflakes go
Scurrying like frightened mice,

Till winter freezes sight and mind
With staring at the shedding skies
And drives me to a house gone blind
With shutters fastened on its eyes.

The Saturday Evening Post, February 2, 1952, p.66

Sudden Shower

Baby with a wrinkled brow
Crying in a tiny basket,
Won't you stop your wailing now
If I should ask it?

Sorrow makes you kick your toes
And flushes pink upon your skin,
Gives you a cherry for a nose
And a trembling chin.

Come here, little thundercloud.
Let me hold you. Stop your storming.
I know why you weep aloud,
And the bottle's warming.

The Saturday Evening Post, January 12, 1952, p.70

April

This is a water-colored time of year
When every day is drenched in dripping rain
And then hung out until rainbows appear
And sunlight spills through door and windowpane,
Sunlight as gentle as a newborn smile
That spreads across a sky of gentian blue
And turns the meadow golden, mile on mile,
And all the naked woods a silver hue.
This is a season when the birds are loud
And winds are crowded with the azure wings
Of jay and bunting and of April cloud
That always hovers on the edge of things.
And this is a month of magic deep at night
When buds unlock themselves in soft moonlight.

The Saturday Evening Post, April 2, 1955, p.75

Sun Sitter

Old Casey's a city-hall sitter by trade.
The north side in summer, of course, for the shade,
And inside in winter to prop up his feet
And bake them all day by the cherry- red heat.
But out again early in April you find him,
Leaving the mayor and council behind him,
And hunting the sunniest spot for his chair,
Then settling down for a month or two there,
As happy and warm as a lily-pad frog
Or leather-back turtle asleep on a log.

―――

The Saturday Evening Post, April 5, 1952, p.79

Polar Expedition

I wrap my little three-year-old
In woolly red against the cold
And from the window watch her go
Exploring in a world of snow
That only magic can arrange:
The hedge an arctic mountain range,
The lilac bush a popcorn tree,
The yard itself a silver sea.

Curious as a climbing kitten,
She hoists herself by boot and mitten
Over a foothill, slick and glazed,
Then tumbles down again, amazed.
Where yesterday the puddles lay
The glaciers trip her up today,
Till, woolly white from toe to chin,
She flounders home to be let in.

***

The Saturday Evening Post

Tom in the Woods

My friend Tom went off to stay
All by himself in a jack-pine wood.
Tall green tree and bright-blue jay
Pleasured him more than people could.
He thought neighbors gladsome things
If they came with beaks and wings.

Not that Tom was sour. I know
Soon as ever he'd hear a joke
From some crackling, sinful crow,
He'd pass it on to a listening oak.
Friendliest man you'd want to meet—
If you wore roots instead of feet.

———

The Saturday Evening Post, March 1, 1952, p.62

Let Me Back In

Devil take such wicked weather!
Snow and sun all mixed together,
Every field a muddy slough
To wet a foot and fill a shoe
And circle any leg that lingers
With a clutch of clammy fingers.

Yet in every patch of shade
Ice in plenty, freshly laid,
To stretch a fellow on his back
And fetch his skull a nasty crack
And make new constellations rise
Brilliantly behind his eyes.

———

The Saturday Evening Post, February 23, 1952, p.124

Keeping Warm

What if the laughing creek is bound
In ice and night is bitter black?
The mole is snug beneath the ground
The mouse is warm in his haystack.

What if the pond is turned to stone
And fields are crusted white and chill?
Beneath the snow the seeds are sown,
Patient as time and living still.

And what if winter stalks the house
And whistles down the fireplace?
We sit here snug as mole and mouse,
With springtime smiling on your face.

———

The Ladies' Home Journal, December, 1951, p.106

Two-Footed Puzzle

Being a two-legged, human thing
That walks about in a suit of clothes,
With neither fur nor claw nor wing
Nor much in the way of teeth and toes,
I live in a cloud of constant wonder,
Puzzling how we keep on going
In spite of snow and sleet and thunder,
War and worry and taxes growing.
Without a tail or a shovel foot
To help us dig as a badger does,
Without a beak, without a root,
Without so much as a gosling's fuzz
Or the feathery raincoat of a duck,
We live, I guess, by love and luck.

The Saturday Evening Post, November 24, 1951, p.86

Autumn Apology

Little skeleton sapling tree
Kidnapped from the woods by me
And hustled home upon my shoulder
Over fence and creek and boulder,
Pray forgive me, if you can,
An erring but repentant man.
I'll dig a dark hole, wide and deep,
With room enough for roots to sleep,
Stretching out their crooked toes
All snug and warm beneath the snows.
I'll see there's a store of drink and meat:
Crumbling, rich black earth to eat,
Draughts of water, cold and clean.
Spring, I swear, shall find you green!

The Saturday Evening Post, October 13, 1951, p.145

Scene Shift

When echoes of summer are dwindled and lost,
The oaks wear red flannels to ward off the frost.
The cattail sticks up like a fireplace poker,
Sumacs are scarlet and maples are ocher,
Gentians are blue in a grassy green niche,
Goldenrod squanders its coin in a ditch,
And katydids fiddle their final debate
As dry as the scraping of chalk on a slate.

———

The Saturday Evening Post, September 15, 1951, p.61

Bright Moment

A red cloud clung to the roof of the south.
The sun lay down in a straw-colored sky.
I sat on the steps with my pipe in my mouth
And watched the gentle blue dusk go by
While Jupiter lighted his lamp in the east.
You were there and the child with her laughter,
And just when I thought of it coming the least,
Up rose the moon, and the stars flew after
Light golden birds in the falling light.
Our hearts welled over like brimming springs,
I laughed aloud and your face grew bright,
And all of us felt the angel's wings
Brushing by in the night.

———

The Saturday Evening Post, September 8, 1951, p.160

Hospital Nursery

Here in this odd, antiseptic place
The babies lie with kicking arms and legs,
Belligerent and vocal, red of face,
In baskets like a batch of new-hatched eggs.

And up and down the hall, we fathers stride,
Cut off from heaven by a windowpane,
Half angry that we cannot get inside,
Half reconciled to wait, and wholly vain.

Impatient for our fledging to be shown
We peek upon the glass, point to the clock,
And when at last the nurse holds up our own,
We crow as loud as any barnyard cock.

The Saturday Evening Post, August 18, 1951, p.81

Highway Report

A half a mile away from us
There lies a ribbon of concrete
Where growling trucks and snarling bus
Go whirling upon rubber feet.

It is an inorganic place,
Insensitive to plow or seed,
And nothing grows upon its face
Immaculate of crop or weed.

But like a whitened scar it splits
The hairy field where wheat is grown;
Its rigid arc of concrete fits
The valley like a great rib bone.

And what it's aimed at I don't know
Nor why a predatory pack
Of metal monsters choose to go
Forever howling forth and back.

⸻

The Saturday Evening Post, June 16, 1951, p.55

Possum County

In Possum County, farms tilt up and down,
The rocks are gray, the earth is copper-brown,
And in the crazy fields the furrows run
Like ladders from your feet up to the sun
Or plunge down into a river bed,
While hills like quiet clouds, lean overhead.

The topsy-turvy farms are ribbon thin,
And rivers fence the quarter sections in.
The tea brown waters purr, white waters shout,
The tumbling, grass-green water hides a trout,
And when corn is in and June commences,
The farmers all go fishing in their fences.

———

The Saturday Evening Post, June 2, 1951, p.42

Windfall of Robins

For near a month we waited here in vain
And stared out at the silver stems of rain,
Till March drew in his breath and pursed his mouth
And blew the robins up from somewhere south,
Square into drizzle, plump into foul weather,
Then left them here to huddle up together,
And gave each one of them a parting cuff
That puffed his feathers out into a muff.
And now each naked branch and swaying twig
Supports a ruffled robin, monstrous big;
And every quaking aspen by the minute
Acquires more robins quaking in it.

The Saturday Evening Post, March 10, 1951, p.98

Time Was

You call this snow, no deeper than your knees?
Why, when I was a boy, it snowed and snowed
And covered up the fence and climbed the trees
And drifted shoulder-high across the road.
I've seen it swallow up the window sill
And pack against the pane and dim the light
And block up every opening until
We lit the lamps at noon as well as night.
You call this snow? This icing on a cake?
I've known it frost this deep a time or two,
With cold enough to make your back teeth ache
And icicles as big around as you.
And snow! We'll never see the like again.
The world has softened up somehow since then.

The Ladies Home Journal, February, 1951, p.113

June Check-Up

It troubles me in early June
To knock off work before I should
And squander half the afternoon
Between the valley and the wood,
But someone has to go and see
That all the schedules have been kept
And rap upon the hollow tree
In case the owl has overslept.
I listen to the thrush's tale
Of speckled eggs begun to crack,
Kneel down to lift a fallen rail
About to break a trillium's back,
And sprawl to let the sun replace
Last summer's freckles on my face.

The Saturday Evening Post, June 12, 1954, p.50

Late Comer

The snow is melting fast away,
The stubble fields are showing through.
I'll give the robin one more day
Before I mark him overdue.
The buds upon the willow tree
Are well-nigh ready to explode.
However could a robin be
Held up so long upon the road?
A love affair in Georgia? Or
Sun-bathing in the Everglades?
He'd better hurry up before
These buds go off like hand grenades.

The Saturday Evening Post, March 6, 1954, p.73

Making My Peace

Now that I've had to spank and scold
And send my naughty one to bed,
Her fairy story left untold,
Her little good-night prayer unsaid,
Her bedtime lullaby unsung,
And all the joy gone out of things,
I feel as mean as if I'd wrung
A bluebird's neck or plucked its wings.
I sink beneath my spirit's weight,
My heart is like a leaden ball,
In vain I try to contemplate
How richly she deserved it all,
Only to go to her at last
And wake her up and hold her fast.

The Saturday Evening Post, February 27, 1954, p.104

Anniversary

Moon by moon and sun by sun
The years have moved into eclipse,
And yet seem only just begun
The vows but fallen from our lips.
I cannot for the life of me
Tell where the drifted days have gone,
Or how that glint of gold could be
A star of evening, not of dawn.
There is some wizardry in this
Too subtle for my wits to trace,
But while I have your mouth to kiss
And sight of your beloved face,
I'll know you always for my bride
And swear the calendars have lied.

Saturday Evening Post, Feb. 13, 1954, p.68

Post-Office Spring

A stranger passing through this winter town
Would never guess our post office to be
A place for spring to set her shy foot down
It has no lawn about it, nor a tree,
Nor any bird but one bedraggled sparrow,
That rides the ridgepole like a weather vane
Blown round and round for lack of any arrow
To point it into wind. The gusts of rain
Shine cold upon slate roof and limestone wall;
And inside, marble floor and iron grille
Deny that they have anything at all
To do with violet or daffodil.
But every March an odd, persistent cheeping
Tunes up behind the doors and window grates
Until the place brims over with the peeping
Of newborn chickens in their shipping crates,
And anybody dropping in can tell
That spring has pecked its way out of the shell.

Ladies Home Journal, February, 1954, p.112

Windjammered

There's something outside bangs at night
Whenever the west wind sets just right,
And something else that squeals and cries
If ever a north wind shakes the skies.
Under the bedroom windowpane
The east wind rattles a clanking chain,
And out in the darkness south wind begs
And wheedles and whines in the windmill legs.
There goes a shutter slamming now,
A banshee rides on the pine-tree bough,
The chimney moans like a lonely cow,
And I'm so weary of wind I vow
I'll trade this place to a mouse or mole
For a chance to live in a soundproof hole.

The Saturday Evening Post, October 17, 1953, p.90

Hidden Fire

Old Henry's head is brown and bare,
And all but innocent of hair,
Save for a tuft at either ear.
His nose comes closer every year
To resting on his pointed chin,
And wrinkles plow their furrows in.

But deep inside of flesh and bone,
Where every man dwells all alone,
The living fire burns as red
In Henry's heart as ever it did,
And flashes from intense blue eyes
To take his children by surprise.

―――

The Saturday Evening Post, November 13, 1948, p.152

Pete

They say when Pete was young, his word
Was deep and slow and seldom heard.
But now, I know, his voice has thinned
Like some old organ out of wind,
And like a winter wind, old Pete
Sends words like dry leaves down the street,
Scraping a story or shrilling a tale
All day long with his foot on a rail,
And never having much to say,
But saying it over again all day,
With a wag and clack of a stiff old tongue
Till the last lamps out and the last dog hung,
And the last ear gone off home to bed,
And the last lip closed, and the last word said.

———

The Saturday Evening Post, April 24, 1948, p.185

Friend in Need

When Tom and his wife had a ten-round fight
And she wouldn't have him inside the house,
He turned up at our place, meek as a mouse,
To see if we'd put him up here for the night.
I told him I'd second him clear to the end
And heated the coffee and poured him a cup,
Then sat down beside him, prepared to stay up
And let him unburden himself to a friend.
He talked of the weather and some of the crop,
The state of the nation, the shortness of cash,
And whether a hen would lay better or stop
With a finger of whiskey stirred into the mash,
And after I'd listened an hour or two
I turned the man out again. Wouldn't you?

The Saturday Evening Post, June 13, 1953, p.123

Footpace

Did heaven make a high-speed flower,
Or horse of more than one horse-power,
Or snail not wise enough to go
Leisurely to and slowly fro?
And did God not make feet for more
Than pressing throttles to the floor?

Go pick daisies, stare at cows,
Sprawl out under the apple boughs,
Stop and sit or kick at a clod,
Amble along at an easy plod.
Life and a journey go so fast
They both should be spun out to last.

The Saturday Evening Post, June 6, 1953, p.112

Spring Flight

My youngest mounts upon her swing
And joyfully does she careen
Between the wet blue sky of spring
And earth's new shining fur of green.

The darting mite has nought to do
With clumsy-footed men like me,
But rides the morning-glory blue
Like hummingbird or bumble-bee.

Her shoes make all the world a drum
To beat upon and soar away,
And like a little pendulum
She measures out the April day.

The Saturday Evening Post, April 25, 1953

Outside and In

Outside tonight the cold is sharp and dry,
With wind to raise a dust of silver snow.
The stars are bright nails driven in the sky,
And a cold penny of a moon hangs low.
The ice is locked on every pond and creek,
And grown upon the branches like a skin.
The night is bitter and the night is bleak,
And nobody is out who can be in.
But here inside, the hickory fire burns,
The baby, nestled in her crib, is snug,
The shadows flicker and the old cat turns
Lazily over on the warm hearth rug,
Content, like me, to purr awhile and hide
From winter, naked as a knife, outside.

The Saturday Evening Post, November 20, 1948, p.188

Baking Day

Today we broil beneath an August sun
That's made a griddle of the chicken run
And turned the barn into a cooking pot
That even mice abandon panting-hot.
It's been a week now since a robin's sung;
The hound dog has unreeled a yard of tongue;
The poor, deep-feathered hens just sit and blink,
Too hot to dip their open beaks and drink.
And I'd lie in the frog pond like a snake,
But clouds of starlings have possessed the boughs,
The pond is crowded full of steaming cows,
And I shall surely bake from skin to gizzard
Unless sheer wishing can provide a blizzard.

―――

The Saturday Evening Post, August 8, 1953, p.93

Well-Mannered

As dainty as a queen in furs,
She sits her down and gently purrs
And dines with busy tongue and jaws.
But then with pussy-willow paws
She tidies up and washes sleek
Her milky chin and velvet cheek.

―――

The Saturday Evening Post, October 18, 1952, p.99

Now Playing

My desk is her wagon, my chair is her horse,
The dining-room table a cave for a fox.
The bathtub a port where a battleship docks,
And I am her personal giant, of course,
Her genie, her slave and her sound-effects man,
Who roars like a lion and grunts like a bear
And initiates guns going off everywhere
With the help of a spoon and an empty tin can.
I don't mind the fuss and I don't mind the bother
Of being a rabbit or wolf or red hen,
But it would be a pleasant surprise now and then
If she'd let me appear in the role of her father.

―――

The Saturday Evening Post, October 4, 1952, p.120

Boy Trap

I've never seen a fox or coon come near
The craftiness a boy has, keeping clear
Of certain kinds of traps, and I should know.
They set enough for me once, long ago.
You can call ducks or dogs, but rarely boys.
They're skilled at hearing chores behind the noise
Of mother on the front porch, wearing out
Her throat and neighbor's patience with her shout.
A dinner bell's a better trick. They'll come
From wonderland for that and stay at home
Until the pie is gone. Then they're gone too,
With lawns unmown and lessons still to do.
A boy's a wild woods thing, no use to scold him
It's only growing up will catch and hold him.

Ladies Home Journal, July, 1952, p.66

May Morning

Below the mountain, wintertime is done,
The bottom land is flooded green, the bees
Crawl through the yellow fingers of the sun
And cling with sticky feet to redbud trees.

Ladies Home Journal, May, 1952, p.154

Two Miracles

Five curious senses and a subtle brain
Fed by the curling tendrils of bright blood,
Depart in death like leaves that come again
When April breathes upon the winter wood.

There are two miracles that I have known—
The pointed leaf that grows upon a thorn,
The brain that flowers on a stem of bone
Return to earth and from the earth are born.

Kaleidograph Magazine, December 1944

Advent

He knocked in anger at the door.
His naked arm was white and thin,
With only the wind as a comforter
And only the night to wrap him in.

His mother drew him through the door,
Out of the darkness, out of harm.
She held the crying mouth to her.
She cradled him till he grew warm.

———

Kaleidograph Magazine, May, 1945

The Backward Look

When I was a boy and the world was new,
Life was as simple as two plus two.
The sun rose up and the sun lay down,
And once in a week we visited town.
Time was content to be time, not space;
Matter a knot that we didn't unlace;
The atom not apt to go off in our face.

But now that my farm is a city of stone
And I but a fabric of wrinkles and bone,
Stiff in the elbow and sore in the knee,
There's scarcely a thing not a puzzle to me.
And most of the facts that I used to declare
Have popped into nothing like bubbles of air
And left me uncertain of what has gone where.

———

The Saturday Evening Post, July 24, 1954, p.64

Going Away

I know she's doing right. It would be wrong
To keep her living here with us forever,
And yet it doesn't seem we've had her long,
And now we'll see her scarce enough or never.
I don't see why they have to move away,
There's our north forty he could have right here.
Too far a piece, clear out to Ioway,
For us to get there even once a year.
And yet she knows her mind, and she's right, too.
A woman's lot is by her husband's side.
We left our home place one time, me and you,
But she's so young, so young to be a bride…
What's that? She's older than you were? Can't be!
You were too young, then, when you married me.

———

The Saturday Evening Post, October 9, 1948 p.118

Color Time

Here's a fine spectacle, everything wearing
Powder and paint and a lot of fandangles.
Wintertime coming and not a thing caring,
Goldenrod tipsy in all the fence angles,
Color enough to fair dazzle your eyes,
With every old sumac a pillar of fire,
And leaves blowing over like bright butterflies,
Carried up higher and higher and higher,
Whirled in a circle of glittering wings,
And laid down again in a carpet of red.
I don't know if I quite approve of such things,
They muddle a man and unsettle his head.
He's apt to get notions that he hadn't ought,
Till winter comes on like a sad second thought.

The Saturday Evening Post, September 25, 1948 p. 136

Night Walk

Too hot for sleep tonight. I think I'll go
Outside and walk awhile to cool off some.
I'll be back pretty soon. Don't wait up, though,
And if I find a breeze, I'll bring it home.
Where shall I walk? Oh, up toward town, I guess.
I like to wander through there late at night
When all the world has finished its business
And gone on home and locked the stores up tight
And left the darkened windows full of stars.
The square is quiet then, and cool as well.
Far off, you hear the rumble of freight cars;
And overhead the heavy courthouse bell,
Half-wakened out of sleep, stirs in the tower
And clears its iron throat to tell the hour.

The Saturday Evening Post, July 10, 1948, p.57

The Treasure Field

When I was ten years old and school was over
And summertime arrived, shining and bright.
The calendar got lost in fields of clover,
And black-eyed Susans flamed up overnight,
Acres of copper coins, new-minted red,
Blossoming treasure, with the sun stopped still
Between the meadow and the milking shed
To let a little miser pick his fill.
And all the summer long, through endless hours
The clouds, full-rigged and towering, sailed by
Like galleons laden with the golden flowers,
Headed for Spain through oceans of blue sky,
While far below, the yellow-shirted bees
Buried their bullion under foaming seas.

The Saturday Evening Post, June 19, 1948, p.133

The Buckler and the Blade

I walked along the edge of land
To hear the solid years roll in:
I saw them break on barren sand
And wash into the sea again.

I stared into the falling sun
And saw the waters of the night
Rise in a thirsty tide upon
The hissing embers of the light.

I live among the hungry men
Who fed themselves upon a lie.
I saw them sicken, one by one,
And one by one I saw them die.

I fled from death as from a thief
And hid me in the woods alone,
Where love was lying under a leaf,
And pity under a weathered stone.

I made a buckler of your heart,
Of your bright tears a shining blade.
We walk together in the dark,
Armored and unafraid.

Kaleidograph. October 1944, p.3

By the Fire

When I'm an old codger I'll sit by the fire
And tell my grandchildren how things used to be,
Back when the sky was a thousand miles higher
And man couldn't fathom the depths of the sea.
When winter was white as a polar bear's grin,
And summer a stove with the sun for a poker,
Spring a rain puddle as deep as my chin,
And fall an explosion of scarlet and ocher.
I'll tell them how all of the women were pretty,
How strong and heroic were all of the men,
And I'll shake my head and pronounce it a pity
That then isn't now and that now isn't then.

―――

The Saturday Evening Post, September 17, 1955, p.54

Night Self

Here is a night of velvet blue,
A star to wish upon, a kiss
Folded up in a thought of you.
What more for me than this?

I was the luckiest of men
In loving you. To hope that such
A magic might occur again
Is asking for too much.

And so I shall stay up awhile
To set the moon upon its shelf,
Put out the star, and try to smile
A little at myself.

The Saturday Evening Post, May 14, 1960, p.128

Winter Carpentry

When windows of my workshop close
Their little eyes beneath the snows
And blizzards wander white and deep,
I light the swinging lamp and keep
On whittling at the weeks until
Time turns into a daffodil.

I saw the minutes up and plane
The hours down till none remain,
And now and then, like chuck or bear,
Go shuffling out to sniff the air,
Then hurry back to sweep away
The shavings of a winter day.

———

The Saturday Evening Post

Second Chorus

Frogs, I hear you in the night,
Crying that the moon is bright.
You're correct, no doubt about it;
Spring is here, but must you shout it
All night long like witless sheep
Baaing when I need my sleep?
Look, I'm in favor of
Lakes and lily pads and love,
Moonlight spilling down like cream
Over every pond and stream
And fringing with a ruff of lace
Every popeyed froggy face,
But now I beg you on my knees
No more encores, if you please.

———

The Saturday Evening Post, May 3, 1958

Cold Reception

You'd think a rabbit would at least
Wait to look a person over
And talk a little, man to beast,
Before retreating into clover,
Showing nothing but the white
Flashing of its own taillight.

It hurts a fellow's feelings to
Pay a call upon a friend,
Expecting to discuss the blue
State of heaven and the end
Purpose of a man or hare,
Only to have him take the air.

―――

The Saturday Evening Post

Autumn Appraisal

I'll grant you that a blood red tree
Fanned out against October sky
Is something that admittedly
Will catch the eye.

And I'll concede that gentians are
Rare as the words to tell their worth,
Each flower a blue and petaled star
Rooted in earth.

Yet in the deep autumnal days
When maples spend their golden leaves
And meadows sleep in a smoky haze
My spirit grieves.

And I'd trade all the gentians in
For sight of a dandelion's honest face
Or the sound of bird song cool and thin
From a nesting place.

The Saturday Evening Post, October 3, 1953, p.55

Man Versus Housekeeping

I find it sad to think the human race is
Condemned to be forever scrubbing dirt
From sticky little hands and grubby faces,
From wall and window, dish and floor and shirt,
From dog and cat and sheets and pillowcases,
The backs of ears, the spotted blouse or skirt,
From all the obvious and obscure places
In this, our life. Oh, I am deeply hurt
When I consider how our time is squandered,
And I am tempted sorely, I confess,
To sign a peace, leave everything unlaundered,
And settle down upon the unwashed mess,
Reclining there in blissful unconcern
Like Nero, while the envious neighbors burn.

―――

The Saturday Evening Post, October 31, 1959, p.72

Winter Woods

There is no movement here at all
But only snow and winter woods,
With never a wing or soft footfall
Among the trees in silken hoods.
I lean upon my ax and wait,
Watching my own quicksilver breath,
And scarcely dare to violate
A silence so akin to death.
I stand and feel my body grow
As quiet as a tree until
My boots seem rooted in the snow,
And it requires an act of will
For me to laugh and choose an oak
And take the first loud-ringing stroke.

The Saturday Evening Post, January 2, 1960, p.43

Visionary

I stand upon the sand and try
To see beyond a certain seam
That binds the ocean and the sky
And separates the fact from dream.
I stare into the well of noon
And cannot plumb the depth of blue.
Oh, must my knowledge end as soon
As all of my perspectives do?
Shall I forever lean on sense
And say so much is true, no more;
Or may I trust the innocence
That whispers of an unseen shore
Where lovers never have to part
And truth is bounded by the heart?

The Saturday Evening Post, February 20, 1960

First Comer

A pitcher plant is very queer
To look at, like a pointed ear
Somehow mislaid by elves. It's odd
To find it cracking concrete sod
So long before the winter's done
Or robins whistle back the sun.
When clouds are full of snow and lie
Most formidably in the sky
And ice has fisted all the stones
And cold has settled in your bones,
Why, then the pitcher plant comes up,
Each one like a crooked cup
Held as if most any minute
April would pour showers in it.

―――

The Saturday Evening Post, March 5, 1960, p.89

Going Back

I felt like Gulliver in Lilliput
When I went back there after all this time.
The place is just as I remembered, but
Diminished from a dollar to a dime.
I reached and picked an apple from the bough
Of that tall tree we were afraid to climb.
The big old belfry tower's tiny now,
And tinkles when the bell begins to chime.
Do you recall the giant who lived within
That corner house we had to pass each day?
I hardly knew him, he had grown so thin,
And his poor dog had dwindled quite away.
But when I met our old school-teacher, then
It was my turn to shrink boy-size again.

―――――

The Saturday Evening Post, September 18, 1948, p. 147

The Defense Rests

But how can you be sure that they're not right
For one another? They're so deep in love,
And he's a good boy. Don't you think you might
Be wrong about them? Are you God above
To make a judgement out of some vast store
Of knowledge I don't have?
How can you tell?
How can you always see behind, before,
Below and up and down and sideways? Well,
I haven't any power such as this.
But last night when I happened to step out
On our front porch, I saw our daughter kiss
This young man you object to, and I doubt
If anything that you or I could do
Would matter much. Now, honestly, don't you?

———

The Saturday Evening Post, November 11, 1959, p.67

The Web of Frost

Spider in your fragile web
Under azure autumn sky,
Fishing in the season's ebb
For a last bluebottle fly,
Are you not aware that soon
In the web of circumstance,
Underneath a waning moon,
You will dance a final dance?
Frost will spin its chilly strand
Round the little world you know,
Binding you within a band
Of iron ice and silver snow.
And there will be no way to break it;
Like us all, you'll have to take it.

―――

The Saturday Evening Post

Time to Go In

Bare is the maple and barren the oak,
Gentian and aster are stripped to the bone,
Chimneys are building their columns of smoke,
Birds have forgathered and gossiped and flown.

All through the valley the fields wear a brown
Ragged old sweater of stubble again
Under a heavy sky bellying down,
Weighted to bursting with burden of rain.

Weary, I turn from the water and mud
And shutter the window and sit by the fire
To bask like a cat till the trees are in bud
And robins come back with cantata and choir.

———

The Saturday Evening Post

The Sleepers and the Sun

When Easter morning on its silver feet
Walks quietly along our sleeping street,
The tulips open up their golden eyes
To see the glory growing in the skies,
And robins hopping on the frosty lawn
Sing anthems of delight in praise of dawn.
But all our shades are drawn against the light,
And in our rooms, with eyelids shuttered tight,
We dream our private dreams and never stir
To watch the miracle outside occur.
Oh, let us waken now, while shadows run
Before the resurrection of the sun,
And give our thanks that it shall rise again
To bring immortal spring to earth and men.

The Saturday Evening Post, April 5, 1958

Midsummer-Night Christmas

High on a hillside that I know
The Christmas trees are growing tall.
The twilight falls as soft as snow,
The moon hangs up a golden ball,
And sleepy robins will not rest
From chorusing in praise of things
Till darkness brims in every nest
And songs are folded up in wings.
Then colored strings of starlight shine
Between the branches and the skies,
The little owls in fir and pine
Burn yellow candles in their eyes,
And katydids wake up the hills
By caroling with whippoorwills.

The Saturday Evening Post

Two-Legged Year

I have four seasons in my blood.
I freeze in winter, thaw in spring,
And brim up in a genial flood
In May when every rooted thing
Is spilling into leaf and bud
And heaven is a lifted wing.

Then, like a river, I recede
And dry up in the summer sun.
The shriveled flower and dusty weed
Are my blood brothers, every one,
And like them all, I run to seed
Before the calendar is done.

———

The Saturday Evening Post, August 31, 1957, p.44

Complaint Department

The goldenrod has come and gone,
The frost has silvered all the lawn,
Gray morning turns to grayer noon
Without a single robin tune,
And though I wish it were not so,
Another week will bring the snow.

I used to think a man a fool
To set his will against the rule
Of calendar or equinox,
But I become less orthodox
As I grow older, and I would
Abolish winter, if I could.

———

The Saturday Evening Post, November 17, 1956, p.125

Thanksgiving Cup

I stand within this field as in a cup,
With all the world around me swirling up
In ridges shaggy with November weather
And brown as old oak leaves or worn leather.
Thanksgiving Day again, and not the first
To find me watching here, nor yet the worst,
For I have known this year the quiet things
That carry men to God on lifted wings:
The golden crown of sun, the tender hour
Of April-scented dusk, the cooling shower
That sifts in summer from a cloudy sieve.
But even more than for all these, I give
My thanks, dear Lord, for love's abiding grace,
Without which earth would be a desert place.

―――

The Saturday Evening Post, November 24, 1956, p.75

Witch

My gown was webbed on a spider's loom,
A graveyard grew me a tufted broom,
A hangman gave me a rope to wind
Round and round whatever I find.

Now when the moon is razor-thin
And curved like a jack-o'-lantern's grin,
And muffled bells of midnight sound,
Black as a bat I spurn the ground.

High where the darkness shows a chink,
My two red eyes will wink and blink,
And if you look, you'll see me soon
Scud like a cloud across the moon.

―――

The Saturday Evening Post, October 28, 1950, p.58

Disturbing the Peace

Pillowed on cloudy drifts of air,
The winds have fallen asleep somewhere
With never a sigh to stir the gray
Curtains that hide the winter day.
Even the whispers of earth have grown
Quiet as clay and still as stone,
With squeaking mice and scratching moles
Curled in a dream in velvet holes.
But under my ax the log of oak
Barks like a dog at every stroke,
Till the sun, at last, comes down to see
Whatever the racket could possibly be,
And the moon climbs up with a sleepy face
To send me home to the fireplace.

———

The Saturday Evening Post, January 12, 1957, p.51

Status Quo

I'm not a man that's overfond of changes.
I get to liking wintertime by May
And worry when October rearranges
The summer in its own haphazard way,
Spilling a pot of paint where it's not wanted,
Kidnapping birds and thinning out the flowers;
But when November comes on, lank and gaunted,
I long for autumn's gold and crimson hours.
And so I pray that when this life is done
And all the final alterations passed,
I can sit down somewhere beneath a sun
Fixed permanently in the sky at last,
And listen to immortal robins call
Among eternal leaves that never fall.

The Saturday Evening Post, November 3, 1956, p.53

Late Lake

Now from quiet shore to shore
Darkness brims the lake once more.
Barking motorboats have each
Bedded down along the beach,
Far above me, fathoms deep,
Stars are turning in their sleep,
And close enough for me to hail
Tacks the moon with yellow sail.
Something ventures near at night
That all day long has taken fright,
And down a rippling, golden aisle
Eternity comes back awhile
To hold the sky and lake and land
An hour or so within her hand.

―――

The Saturday Evening Post, August 10, 1957, p.80

Stubborn

Grandpa, admit it. This is a sad farm,
This valley embraced by a mountain's stiff arm.
A spade stuck in anywhere grates on the stone,
The skin of your garden can scarce hide the bone,
The fields run to bindweed and buckhorn and dodder
And quack grass and thistles and prickly fodder.

The pig is all spareribs. There's nothing that thrives.
The cow's two hipbones are like sharp pruning knives.
The hen's but a hunger between beak and toes,
And mortgages gobble whatever crop grows.
Come away. Give it up. Let the bank have the land.
But why you won't do it? I can't understand!

―――

The Saturday Evening Post, August 22, 1959, p.66

Summer Midnight

How quietly the summer sleeps tonight.
The darkness and the silence wrap it round;
A single star lifts up a point of light;
One cricket stirs and scratches into sound;
And half a house away, I hear the clock
Still gossiping in undertones with time,
Explaining it in terms of tick and tock,
And bidding heaven wait for bells to chime.
Far off, a farm dog startles, and his bark
Plunges in silence like a shooting star;
And keeping track of time along the dark,
The whisper of a train comes from afar.
Then slumber seals the night, and sound is gone
Until the drums of rain wake up the dawn.

The Saturday Evening Post, July 9, 1949, p.86

Forsaken Lane
and
Empty Church

The rutted lane, nailed down by sapling birch
And fierce with berrybush and thistle head --
You wouldn't think it carried folks to church
But once upon a time, that's where it led.
It carries its own jungle now on top
And looks like any other old hedgerow.
See how the hazel bushes wind and stop
Down yonder where a roof and steeple show?

Why yes, the church is there, still listening for
The sound of buggy wheel or clop of hoof,
But weathered silver now with gaping door,
A bell tower loud with bees, a moss-rug roof.
Wild roses climb the clapboards, tiny feet
Of morning-glories cross the old doorsill,
And from a dozen nests, where rafters meet,
A choir of robins praises heaven still.

―――

The Saturday Evening Post, June 20, 1953

The Sleepy Dance

At evening when the drowsy sun
Lies pillowed on a cloudy sky
And little babies have begun
To yawn and rub a sleepy eye,
I pick my youngest up and hold her,
Soft as any feathered thing,
With her head upon my shoulder
For a bedtime rock and sing.
Round about the rug we waltz
To listen to each other croon,
And for a moment heaven halts
The blossoming of star and moon
And hushes up the birds and keeps
Night quiet till my baby sleeps.

The Saturday Evening Post, May 8, 1954, p.58

Midnight Zero

Where snow-encrusted poplars lift
Their white arms to the naked stars,
I walk upon a winter drift
Beneath the open eye of Mars.

Here is a loveliness as bare
And brutal as a sharpened knife.
The earth a web of ice, the air
A razor at the throat of life.

Uneasily I turn about
And make for home and firelight,
While overhead the trees cry out
Against the bitter weight of night.

―――
The Saturday Evening Post, Jan. 14, 1956, p.83

Time Bomb

A gray cocoon hung in a tree,
Quite insulated from the pinch
Of circumstance; a tiny free
And independent cubic inch
With business of its own; a womb
No bigger than a baby's thumb;
A temporary little tomb
Until the Easter angels come.
And so I broke a silver twig
To ease tomorrow from its socket,
Went off feeling somehow big
With resurrection in my pocket,
And hurried home to you to bring
This promissory note of spring.

The Saturday Evening Post, March 26, 1960, p.58

The Springtime Pig

Today when sudden thaw had sent
A southern sun to fire the sky,
The old hog hobbled from the sty
Where he had long lain winter-pent.

His little eyes were chilly stones,
His hide a frozen stubble field,
The washboard of his ribs revealed
How frost had settled in his bones.

Now wearily, he laid him deep
Within a puddle of the sun
And grunted thanks for winter done
And shut his lids and went to sleep.

The Saturday Evening Post, March 21, 1953, p.144

A Northern View

I doubt if I could love a land
Forever cupped in summer's hand,
Where winter never shook the nights
With hammers of the northern lights
Or dressed the trees in linen clothes
Or sent a frost to bite my toes.

The heavy-lidded, swarthy South,
Where poppies lift a sleepy mouth
And stars hang ripe as golden fruit
Is something scarcely meant to suit
A blue-jawed Yankee like myself,
Grown on a mountain's granite shelf.

And then what Southern spring could show
The crocus candle-flames in snow?
Or plunging horses of the hills
With manes of yellow daffodils?
Or cold, blue-melted lakes that lie
Like fallen fragments of the sky?

The Saturday Evening Post, Feb. 26, 1955, p.47

Launching Platform

A wind came roaring up today
And tossed a thousand hats away,
Trampled earth and shook the sky.
Blew the tumbling robins by,
And turned a clothesline full of things
Into frantic, flapping wings.

Far above our upward faces
Fly the sheets and pillowcases,
Soaring shirt tails, bits of lace,
Headed straight for outer space
And circled by a single bright
Long red flannel satellite.

———

The Saturday Evening Post, March 30, 1957, p.48

Star Swing

When I came courting, you and I would swing
Deep in the shadows of your father's porch,
To watch the sun lay down his smoky torch
And see the moon fly like a dove's white wing.
And somehow that old porch swing's slatted bars
Rose up into the magic night till soon
We rode upon the shoulders of the moon,
We swung content among the cloudy stars.

Of course, my love, that's been some time ago;
We walk in daylight now on sunny earth
And deem a clothesline full of diapers worth
More than the glittering starlight's silver snow.
Yet in the blue night, when along the south
A new moon sails its creamy cockleshell,
The same old porch swing suits us very well,
The same old magic rests upon your mouth.

―――

The Saturday Evening Post, Oct. 20, 1951, p.149

Moon Walking

The moon has a broad, good-natured face,
And wrapped to the chin in cool blue night
He walks his beat across our place
To try each door with a stick of light.

Down by the creek a tipsy frog
Hiccups to see his lantern shining;
Here in the house he prods the dog
Into a dream and sets him whining.

Above our spring he bends to take
A long look in its silver cup,
Then saunters off to touch awake
Each mockingbird and tune him up.

The Saturday Evening Post, July 25, 1953, p.102

In the Hayfield

This, I thought, is a pleasant thing,
To swing a scythe while robins sing,
And shave a field as smooth as skin
And breathe the smell of cut hay in.
A pleasant thing, a job of worth,
Being a barber to the earth,
With a two-foot razor blade to pass
Whispering through the whiskered grass.
Thus I rocked along, content,
Half asleep and innocent
Of any motive but the best,
And so unroofed a rabbit's nest.
There lay bare babies in a heap.
The scythe had missed them in its sweep,
But suddenly the sky turned black.
I knelt and put the babies back,
And kneeling there, I heard the thunder
As angels noted down my blunder.

―――――

The Saturday Evening Post, June 17, 1950, p.126

The Fragile Time

Step softly in this gold and crimson wood.
The time is brittle and the fragile sky
Hangs like a single pane of glass that could
Be shattered by a football or a cry.
Above us tremble painted-china leaves;
The air transparent as a crystal lens
Refracts the light and angles it and weaves
A rainbow out of brilliant odds and ends.
Within a week this linden, tall and proud,
With rounded body like a golden cloud,
This sumac flickering with scarlet flames,
Will both be bare and blackened wooden frames.
Stripped by the frozen fire of the frost.
Step softly, softly, lest a leaf be lost.

―――

The Saturday Evening Post

Better Come In

Now that the final curling leaf
Has left the elm and slanted down,
The sky is gray as an old man's grief
And earth is leather-brown.

Here is poverty bare and grim:
A stalk of tarnished goldenrod,
An empty nest on an empty limb,
And an empty milkweed pod.

Rain comes down in a silver blur
As cold as spray from arctic seas,
And with it a northern wind to stir
The naked spars of trees.

The last few robins disappear,
The last fields turn to stubble,
This is no time to linger here
With all outdoors in trouble.

We'll sweep the hearth and be about
Building a fire to last the night,
And fence the death and darkness out
With pickets of scarlet light.

The Saturday Evening Post, October 22, 1949, p. 45

Nativity

Zero cold it was, with wind around,
And like an hourglass of blue starlight
Orion stood above the frozen ground,
Timing the passage of the winter night.
"I'll call the doctor now," I said. "We'll go
Over there right away." Your mother smiled,
And out we went upon the crusted snow,
Under the watching stars, to find a child.
All night and all day long, and when the skies
Darkened again, my courage was undone,
But still I saw within your mother's eyes
Faith burning steady as another sun.
And then you came to let my fear depart,
And joy sang like a robin in my heart.

                  The Saturday Evening Post, Dec. 25, 1948, p.57

An Old Song for a New Year

To love I pledge a brimming glass
Now that the year has shrunken small.
Without the lover and his lass,
Who would want a year at all?

If love were not, then better far
For me to find a wave of night
And drift upon it like a star
Across the darkened infinite.

What are the sun and moon to me
But light from your beloved face?
Without your eyes for me to see,
This earth would be a desert place.

So let the old year roll behind,
And ring the new from north to south,
And may the bells of midnight find
My mouth upon your mouth.

———

The Saturday Evening Post, Dec. 30, 1950, p.72

Valentine

You cannot see behind the moon,
Or put your finger on a star,
Or cause the sun to set at noon,
Or cage a genie in a jar.
You cannot call the wind, or make
A rain of fire in the night,
Or find a rainbow's end, or take
A lump of coal and scrub it white.
This is a sorry thing to be
Unable to catch quicksilver,
Or cast a net upon the sea
And hold a wave a prisoner,
But more than these, you understand
How my heart beats within your hand.

―――

The Saturday Evening Post, Feb. 12, 1949, p. 106

Spring Fires

All winter long, I walked and thought
Here is a good land come to naught,
Scarred by frost and whipped by sleet
And chilled beneath the snow's white feet.
But when I looked today, I found
Green fire growing in the ground.
The pointed tips of wheat arose
Like candles lit in gleaming rows;
The ash and oak and elm became
Tall silent columns of green flame;
And even more now upon these hills
Burn the yellow daffodils,
And dandelions like embers glow,
Golden in the melting snow.

———

The Saturday Evening Post, March 12, 1949, p.146

Morning after Storm

Fire flicked a crooked tongue
And licked the fingers of an oak.
Then from darkness thunder spoke,
And all night long the roof has sung
Over and over the same refrain
Under the gray batons of rain.

Now, like a lovely woman, comes
Morning with her silver eyes.
From her footprints flowers rise,
From her hand a fat bee hums
And all around her robins shout
And fluff bedraggled feathers out.

The Saturday Evening Post

First Picnic

There's still a patch or two of snow
That shrinks and withers by the minute,
And if a north wind chose to blow
It might well have a sharp tooth in it.
But what of that? A fig for winter's
Scraps and leavings, when the sun
Pricks the earth with bright green splinters
And the brooks all melt and run!
We'll picnic in a grassy cup
That gathers yellow noonday up
And hold it in a bowl of light
Till dandelions pop into sight.
Like pennies on a green banknote
Or buttons on spring's overcoat.

―――

The Saturday Evening Post, April 10, 1954, p.114

Sky Bull

It's good to see the sun again
Pawing up the clouds, his eye
Glaring down at earth and men
From pastures of the April sky.

I like to watch him grazing over
Melting valleys of the air,
Like a young bull in the clover,
Bidding wintertime beware.

And I'll get up before the light
To find him, full of lusty pride,
Charging up the hill of night
And shouldering the stars aside.

―――

The Saturday Evening Post, April 9, 1960, p.88

The Rooster and the Sun

I lose myself in wonder at the cock
Who blows his feathery trumpet every dawn
Merely to call a sleep-besodden flock
Of bleary hens to breakfast on the lawn.

Indignantly he shrills a blast of warning
To let the harem know how chicken hawks
Can plunge in seconds down the cliffs of morning
From heaven to where the plumpest pullet walks.

Then loudly does he hail the golden sun,
As if it were a great egg he had laid,
And bids his family cackle, peck and run
Beneath another day that he has made.

———

The Saturday Evening Post, April 7, 1956, p.112

Rain Loose

Over the shutter, the sill and the pane
Gallop the dapple-gray legs of the rain,
To stamp in the grass and to strike at the roof,
To splash in the puddle with silver-shod hoof,
To drum on the barn and to scatter beyond
The garden, the meadow, the dancing duckpond.

Runaway, runaway, never a doubt,
Frightened by thunder and racing all out,
With a rattle of hoofs and a roll of an eye,
Leaping the fences of earth and the sky,
Trampling wheat till it's broken and bowed,
And striking the fire from iron-gray cloud.

———

The Saturday Evening Post, August 25, 1951, p.123

The Broken Night

I don't know if a cat on cushioned paws
Crept, grinning and soft-bellied through the grass,
Or whether a horned owl, with curling claws
And beak as terrible as broken glass,
Came gliding down the darkness, but last night
I heard the brittle silence shiver and crack,
A nesting bird's abrupt squawking of fright,
Shrilling and wild—and then the hush came back.

I'll grant you that to damn a prowling cat
Or try an owl for murder is to blame
Ice for its iciness and argue that
A fire has no right to be a flame.

What then? I cannot hear the night cry out
And turn myself, grunting, again to sleep.
I am the bird that cats have crept about,
Above my heart the wings and talons sweep,
For I, too, am a nester on the ground,
Wrapped up in swaddlings of the velvet air.
This broken night that splinters into sound
Flays off my covering and strips me bare.

―――

The Saturday Evening Post, May 12, 1951, p.96

Deep Summer

The dusty vines hang heavy on the fences;
The poppies flame along the cobbled wall;
We wade so deep in summer that our senses
Can scarcely credit wintertime at all.
The hot, blue valleys of the summer sky
Slope down above us near enough to burn
Our fingers on the sun. The days go by
As easy as a dream, the stars return
Like lanterns hung out lower every night,
And every night the tipsy bullfrogs sing
A booming baritone in soft starlight,
While locusts buzz and fiddle on one string
And fireflies strike matches in the wheat.
Winter is dead! No snow can ever spill
Out of a bruised black cloud again, nor sleet,
Nor sleds cascade again down frozen hill.

———

The Saturday Evening Post, August 11, 1951, p.105

Windy Summit

All day long above our hill
The humming wind has hurried by,
And now in sleep we hear it still
Striding through the midnight sky.

The house thrusts up a wooden shoulder
Into west wind day and night
And splits air like a river boulder
Combing water black and white.

It's like a lick of salt high hung
For curling tongues of wind to suck,
Or like a hollow banjo strung
With twanging wires for the wind to pluck.

And if the singing night grows still,
We start awake and wonder why
And stir uneasily until
The wind takes up its lullaby.

The Saturday Evening Post, Nov. 17, 1951, p.147

The Robin Tree

Where chilly robins huddle now
Along each windy, naked bough,
The casual eye can almost see
Red apples in a barren tree
And, scattered here and there below,
Windfalls of robins in the snow.

It is a curious sort of thing
To hear a flock of apples sing,
And now especially out of reason
In such a bitter, frosty season.
High time, don't you think, for May
To clarify all this some way?

———

The Saturday Evening Post

The Trap

I've never seen a March like this before,
When summertime walks up and down the street,
And bees come buzzing in the open door;
With air like incense, rich and blossom-sweet,
And all the trees dressed out in sticky buds,
And grass and clover deep enough to mow;
Mayflowers trailing soft along the woods,
And tulips bright as soldiers in a row.
I want to cry, "Go back, go back, go slow!
You are too credulous, too trusting. Hark!
The winter stirs. I hear it. Heed and go
Back underground, back into root and bark.
Be wise, be hard; and if you would endure,
Before you give yourself away, be sure."

The Saturday Evening Post, March, 1946

Full Circle

A year ago, that crimson star
Hung its lamp on the pasture bar,
And off to the north where ridges rise
The great bear showed his yellow eyes.
I saw Pegasus, then as now,
Kicking free of a hickory bough,
And deep in the dark blue web of things
Saturn spun on golden rings.
Night is a dream of starry light,
And day is a silver seam of night,
And what is time but a stunning thief
To hide a flower or lift a leaf,
Or steal a year away so sly
That no theft shows upon the sky?

―――

The Saturday Evening Post, Nov. 5, 1949, p.116

Kathy

Our baby is no bigger than a minute.
She curls inside my arms as though it were
A proper armchair with enough room in it
For one or two more just the size of her.
She has a way, besides, of squeezing up
And folding little arms and legs together
Till she could fit inside a china cup;
It wouldn't have to be a big one either.
Kathy's toes are fringed with tiny toes,
And her two hands behave like butterflies
That flutter round the bud of her pink nose
And over the blue petals of her eyes.
And, all in all, it's hard to figure why
So small a mite should have so large a cry.

———

The Saturday Evening Post, July 17, 1948

Hall of Giants

The heavy punch presses are bound in bright steel
And bolted to timber embedded in rock.
One-legged giants, they stamp with a shock
That a maple tree half a mile distant can feel.
Crumbs of red copper pile up by their feet
And slices of iron are crunched in their jaws.
By daylight or midnight with never a pause
The stamping goes on and the great presses eat,
And the sound of their feeding is something to hear
And the sight of their teeth a persuasion to fear,
Till a man at the end of his shift wants to run
To a quiet green field and the silence of sun,
With the hush of forever bent over his head
And the mute earth beneath him for pillow and bed.

The Saturday Evening Post, May 24, 1952, p.115

Courthouse Square

Uptown there's not a lot of living matter
Left beside the busy people there.
Of course, the pigeons raise a kind of clatter
And clap blue wings together in the air,
And there's a patch of sorry grass between
The cast-iron soldier and the stone marine,
With, now and then, a horse to stand hipshot
Beside a parking meter's grinning slot.

But by and large, it's gasoline and steel
That give a roar and sputter to uptown.
The hoof has yielded to the racing wheel,
A thousand tail pipes bellow up and down,
And it's a small wonder that a staring pig,
Transported through this iron whirligig,
Squeals from his truck in terror and dismay.
He's not the only one to feel that way.

The Saturday Evening Post, Dec. 15, 1951, p.125

Thick Tonight

The valley is a cloudy cup,
The lower field a steaming bog,
And smoky tides are rolling up
To wrap the house in waves of fog,
With silver flowing on the grass
And lapping doors and window glass.

I step out of the lighted room
And stare into the curling mist.
A branch floats like a witch's broom,
A bush holds up a giant fist,
And drippings from the gutter sound
Like ghostly feet upon the ground.

The Saturday Evening Post, Sept. 1, 1951, p.63

Mountain Farm

It's cheap. You can afford it, like as not.
Before you buy, though, let me tell you what
The farm is like. You'll find yourself alone
All year upon a mountain of your own.
Nobody will come near to call your name
But wind, and wind will always be the same,
Cascading down the mountain to the sea
Like water running, wild and white and free.
You will be drunken with the wind, and when
You go to town to seek out other men
You'll find them curious and feel them stare
To see you lean on the wind no longer there.
You'll find rocks plentiful and topsoil thin
And bones of mountains showing through the skin.

The Prairie Schooner, Spring, 1948

Ethan Benderby

Old Ethan Benderby came down the road
Last night, tacking under the August stars.
And carrying, as always, quite a load
Of liquid cargo picked up at the bars
In Morganburg. He lives a mile from town
And strides home straddling the curving world,
A giant peering curiously down
From heights incredible, his fingers curled
About the cornice of the moon. His feet
Blind wanderers upon the distant earth.
A free soul disembodied and complete,
Now witnessing a galaxy's bright birth,
Now fallen prone and staring at a clod,
Now talking to himself, and now to God.

The Prairie Schooner, Spring, 1948

Pumpkin Time

Now all unquiet things have fallen still.
The bird song dies away, the insect humming
Grows oddly silent on the brown-skinned hill.
We listen for the tread of winter coming
And hear instead our own boots in the stubble,
Scratching as we crunch our way around
The orange pumpkins, each a monstrous bubble
Somehow blown up and stranded on the ground.
Tier on tier, the ridges rise away;
Trough by trough, the valleys angle down,
And every ridge is hazed a smoky gray
And every valley stained a coffee brown,
While off on the very edge of things
A pair of mountains lift their soft-blue wings.

―――

The Saturday Evening Post, Nov. 3, 1951, p.54

Spring Morning

This valley holds the morning in a cup.
Excess of sunlight brims the mountains up,
And rolls white radiance upon the floor
Between the hills. At every farmer's door
The morning screams and stamps a silver hoof.
Slate fires burn on every farmer's roof,
And sunlight crows the morning like a cock,
And mountains ring the morning like a clock.
Come, slug-a-bed, you hear the sunlight rapping
Upon dark shutters. Get up from your napping.
Come walk with me to wade in white sunrise,
And feel the morning tugging at your thighs
And watch the mountain shed its winter skin.
Come out, come out, and drink the morning in.

———

The Atlantic Monthly, June, 1945

Firewood

If you want the fire tonight, you'll chop some wood
This afternoon before the early dark.
Northeast in the far orchard there's a good
Stand of old trees with scaly tinder-bark.
Dead limbs, green-lichened, ready for the fire,
Grown up with poison oak, though -- mind your hands.
Look for bright berries, vines as tough as wire,
And when you see it, leave it where it stands.
What kind? Why, apple trees, past bearing now.
Lord knows how old they are. Sometimes in spring
A few white blossoms creep along the bough.
None last year though. The only blessed thing
That orchard's good for is to burn at night.
So get along now. Hurry while there's light.

The Atlantic Monthly, Feb. 1946

Involuntary

I have grown intimate with death
And sat beside him, knee to knee,
And with him measured out the breath
Of her whose love was life to me.

What have I this Thanksgiving Day
But blackened ashes of a flame?
How can I lift my hands to pray
In gratitude and not in blame?

And yet I *will* give thanks.
My love for this earth verges onto lust.
And I will sing to Him above
Because my heart declares I must.

―――

The Saturday Evening Post, Nov. 30, 1957, p.53

The Quiet Answer

Come rest an hour, I said. The work is done.
The corn is green and tall as sapling trees.
The pasture land is flooded gold with sun,
And bluegrass laps the cattle to their knees.
Let us be lazy now and take our ease;
Sprawl under apple trees and watch the fruit
Slow ripening, and listen to the bees
Go purring home from clover with their loot.
How long has summer been? At least forever.
We must have dreamed of winter long ago.
These leafy apple boughs above have never
Glittered in ice or webbed themselves in snow.
But even as I spoke, a leaf replied
And fluttered down to show me that I lied.

———

The Saturday Evening Post, Aug. 20, 1949, p.43

In the Hayloft

What's this rolled up in a wisp of straw?
The tiniest mouse I ever saw,
Curled up tight and pink as a rose,
With pin-point eyes and pinhead nose,
Spanking new and shiny clean
And just the size of a jelly bean.
But what to do with a baby mouse?
Mice aren't welcome in the house,
And in the barn the tomcats stalk,
And in the field the swinging hawk.
Rats would relish such a soft
Morsel left in their hayloft.
Would that I'd never found the bare
Helpless creature curled up there.
One finger snap would snuff him out
Against my thumb and end this doubt,
And yet…how rare a pinch of life --
I'll pocket him and ask my wife.

The Saturday Evening Post, July 15, 1950, p.94

Mole

At dusk when I put up my rake
And stood to watch the dappled sky,
The grass lay level as a lake
And pleased the eye.

But when a robin called me out
At sunup to behold the change,
I found these valleys sprawled about
This mountain range.

You wouldn't think one mole could make
A lunar landscape of the lawn;
More like an overnight earthquake
Had come and gone.

And so it's war. Each afternoon
I'll roll his ramparts under clover
But every night beneath the moon
He'll build them over.

And not till earth is sealed in stone
And frost has bound it rim to rim,
Will he leave it or me alone,
Or I leave him.

———

The Saturday Evening Post, May 27, 1950, p.130

Sound Track

I relish the sound of a bubbling pot,
The chunking bite of an ax in wood,
The flames that hiss at a hickory knot,
And hens that cluck to a peeping brood,
Roosters trumpeting clear and strong,
A purring cat, a bedtime yawn,
And squeaking wagon wheels of song
Made by the blackbirds on the lawn.
But save me from the midnight train
That whistles to the waiting heart
And wails desire into the brain
And steals the listener far apart
From thought of home or love of kin
And leaves goose prickles on his skin.

The Saturday Evening Post, August. 5, 1950, p.106

Crisis Averted

When I walked to the store today
I met a bulldog on the way
That glowered at me dark and grim
As if I had affronted him.

The path is narrow there. I found
No way to ease myself around
This animated, black bear trap
Without inviting it to snap.

It seemed a time for me to wait
A more propitious turn of fate,
And so I stood in quaking calm
Before the squat, four-legged bomb.

And in all likelihood I'd be
There yet, and so, no doubt would he,
If heaven hadn't sent a cat.
But heaven did, and that was that.

The Saturday Evening Post, July 10, 1954, p.86

Empty Woodchuck

The chuck came out to take the sun
This morning after his long night.
Beside the stump he sat upright
And watched me work. I had begun
To spade the garden up, a sight
That likely was a welcome one.

He looked as lanky as a hound.
The sleek rotundity of fall
That made him such a furry ball
Had somehow melted underground
And left him with no paunch at all
To clasp his little paws around.

His cupboard must be nearly bare:
A wrinkled root, a cherry stone,
And last October's marrow bone
Well-seasoned by the frosty air.
This summer, with the turnips grown,
We'll both sit down to better fare.

―――

The Saturday Evening Post, April 26, 1952, p.147

The Flower Eater

Above the cow the sky is blue
And honey-sweet with clover smell,
But all she does is pluck and chew
And play ding-dong on her cowbell.
Beneath her nose the buttercup,
The daisy and the bluet rise,
But all she does is eat them up
Or stare at them with vacant eyes.
Tell me now, old lump of leather,
If you find the season sweet
And take delight in bright June weather
Golden as the flowers you eat,
Don't you think the thing to do
Would be to moo a thankful moo?

———

The Saturday Evening Post

Elbow Room

There was a golden age, I have been told,
When earth had space enough and more to hold
Each Tom and Dick and Harry and their dreams
Without the slightest straining of her seams,
A time when every land from sea to sea
Had elbow room for men like you and me
To shake opinions in. Well, I confess
I'm not one for this togetherness
That cans us like sardines from pole to pole
And packs us willy-nilly, cheek by jowl,
Until a man may scarcely sneeze
Without offending the antipodes,
Or yawn and stretch as widely as he can
For fear of poking ribs in Pakistan.

The Saturday Evening Post, Feb. 25, 1961, p.81

The Winter Crop

The wind fell and the frozen night
Turned quiet as an old man's thought.
Snow in the valley lay blue-white,
And on the pond the ice grew taut.
"We'd better get the gear together,"
Grandpa said, "to help us take
A crop of February weather
Off the acre of our lake."
And all day long, with pike and wedge,
Saw and spudding iron and sledge,
We cut the winter into clean
Shining blocks of blue and green
And hauled it off upon a sleigh
To hoard against a summer day.

The Saturday Evening Post, Feb. 16, 1957, p.109

In the Doorway

Tonight you came out of the snow and stood
Framed for a moment in the open door,
Stars scattered back of you, lamplight before,
And darkness round your hair like a blue hood.
How can I tell you? How bewitch a brood
Of clucking words into jeweled metaphor?
You came like one I long had waited for
In dream, in memory, in enchanted wood.
You stood there lovely as embodied song
Until you saw some token in my face
Of how I felt, and asked me what was wrong.
I had no words to tell you for a space
How my own wife, whom I had loved so long,
Seemed like a sudden angel on the place.

                  The Saturday Evening Post, Dec. 17, 1949, p.46

Recital

Little ballerina, stop
Spinning like a scarlet top.
Let me look at you to see
How you could belong to me.

Here I am as heavy-footed
As an oak tree iron-rooted.
While you point *en relevé*
Or flicker in a *fouetté*.

Firefly in red tutu,
Miracles may well be true
Since it's a fact that I became
Father to a candle flame.

―――

The Saturday Evening Post, Oct. 6, 1956, p.124

Thaw

That dripping noise you asked about --
It's not in the house, but out
By the roof where sunlight tickles
Long white ribs of old icicles.

Come out here and have a look
At the glinting pasture brook.
That's not ice that glitters bright:
The water shed its skin last night.

Everywhere beneath the sun
Sparkling little rivers run,
And there upon the melting snow
A robin plays his piccolo.

———

The Saturday Evening Post, Feb. 24, 1951, p.98

A Carol for Two Voices

How far away, how far away
Is peace upon this Christmas Day?
Oh, farther still than men may go
By death-cold sea or bone-white snow.

What of good will among all men?
How long till then? How long till then?
Oh, longer yet than you or I
Shall walk beneath this winter sky.

Then where is Christ and where is love?
I see no star of hope above.
Has even He withdrawn apart?
Look in your heart, look in your heart.

———

The Saturday Evening Post, Dec. 27, 1952, p.70

City: Day's End

Earthward down a shaft of steel
We drop within a gilded car
That plummets from a spinning reel
As swiftly as a shooting star.
We step out into shouting streets
Where trolleys swim like iron whales,
Their bellies lined with crowded seats.
We travel home on crying rails;
And safe at last in cliffs of stone,
We shed our nylon skins to creep,
Brain and body, blood and bone,
Into a quiet crack of sleep.

———

The Saturday Evening Post, September 13, 1952, p.145

New Lamb in March

Insubstantial pinch of fluff,
What makes you think you weigh enough
To keep from being blown away
By the first wind that roars today?

This bully braggart of a season,
Cold and windy out of reason,
Fit for neither ewe nor ram,
Is no month for a little lamb.

———

The Saturday Evening Post, March 4, 1950, p.98

Black Angus

On May nights when the moon is full
And apple blossoms scent the dark,
The curly-headed Angus bull
Shrugs a hide like hickory bark.

He lifts his great head like a cloud
And lurches to barn-window height
Upon four knotted legs half bowed
Beneath a ton of living night.

The moon glints on a golden ring
In nostrils like a flaring rose
And brushes with its silver wing
The shaggy column of his nose.

The Angus stares in stolid wonder
Out of eyes turned ember hot,
And then like rolling summer thunder
Bellows for he knows not what.

The Saturday Evening Post, May 19, 1951, p. 166

Love Song

They told me love was like a flame
That flickered out, or like a bird
That flew away when winter came,
His song forgotten and unheard.

They said love vanished like a cloud
Before a wind that walked the sky,
Or disappeared into a crowd
Of other loves. I say they lie.

If love were of such shoddy stuff
As most of its detractors are,
The sun would cool off soon enough
And earth become a shooting star.

Believe me, this is truth alone:
Deep-rooted in the heart of God,
True love will outlast flesh and bone
As sure as earth outlasts a clod.

The Saturday Evening Post, April 22, 1950, p.148

The Watcher

Whenever I walk down her street, I find
The sly old face behind a window blind,
Half hidden, half revealed, one bright black eye
Sharp as a needle point to prick and pry.
She has a fine front porch. Why doesn't she
Come out and sit down on it openly
To look upon the world direct and bold
Instead of webbed up in a curtain fold?
God grant me this, that I may never peer
Through peepholes, half concealed from what I fear.
It's hard enough to see where candor lies
Behind the lidded curtains of our eyes
When we stare at each other face to face,
Not winking from a mouse's hiding place.

―――

The Saturday Evening Post, April 11, 1953, p.126

Deep-Rooted

I've known that oak tree since its birth,
When first it split the ground to climb
Steadily upward from the earth,
Cradled in wind and nursed by time.
And if my flesh were living wood
And I had talons like a tree
To grip the world itself, I could
Begin to share your faith in me.

But, dearest, you must surely know
I am made of no lasting stuff;
The wind may bend me with a blow,
And time shall fell me soon enough,
That I have weathered storm so far
Is by no virtue of my own;
The roots that hold me upright are
Deep buried in your love alone.

The Saturday Evening Post, Oct. 1, 1955, p.123

October Meeting

Beneath a sugar-maple tree
Where I chopped at a fallen limb,
A squirrel sat up to look at me
And I sat down to look at him.

We were unlike in many ways
And yet we had a world to share
Of red and yellow autumn days
And needle-sharp October air.

And, take us all in all, we were
Confronted by a like concern,
He with growing winter fur
And I with finding wood to burn.

———

The Saturday Evening Post, Oct. 8, 1955, p.49

The End of It

Now comes the time of ending, every tree
Has crackled into crimson leaf or gold
And flamed an autumn through for you and me,
Walking the woods together, to behold.
The oaks have strutted like great crimson cocks
Parading down October's azure haze,
With maples pasturing in shaggy flocks
Like golden sheep upon the sun-deep days.
But now the rain with flashing silver shears
Strips off the feathers of each cockerel oak
And fleeces maples bare. The sky appears
A troubled wilderness of cloud and smoke,
With one bird tossed upon it headlong south,
Blown like a leaf by winter's bitter mouth.

The Saturday Evening Post, Oct. 31, 1953, p.64

Home by Starlight

A chilly walk and far to go,
And dark so I can hardly see
Whether a blot is a barn or tree
And whether a drift is high or low.
Plenty of light in heaven, though --
Look at the Dipper upside down,
Spilling stars from here to town,
And old Orion stuck in snow.
I'll have a moon in another mile
And a shadow then to walk beside
Keeping me company, stride by stride,
By frozen creek and icy stile
And under starlight blazing blue,
All the way home to the fire and you.

———

Ladies' Home Journal, Jan. 1951, p.128

Dark Visitor

I wish to God I knew some place
Where I could lock my love away
Secure from death, whose quiet face
Looked in upon us yesterday.
But lovers have nowhere to hide:
We cannot creep beneath a leaf
Or find a crack and slip inside
Beyond the fingers of this thief.
No bolted door, no cunning mesh
Of woven steel, no wall of stone
Can shield the petal of the flesh
Or save the living stem of bone.
But only this—if we possess
A love as strong and sure as death,
What matters one heartbeat the less?
One pitiable pinch of breath?
Death cannot grasp the sun, nor cup
His bony hand about the sea,
Nor take love but to lift it up
From earth into eternity.

The Saturday Evening Post, July 26, 1952, p.104

Spring Questioning

I've seen it happen enough by now
To know what's coming and know it well.
But when a blossom breathes out of a bough
As horny and tough as a turtle's shell,
Or a mud cocoon splits open wide
To free the magic curled inside
That flies like a leaf on a golden pin,
Or I see an acre, bald and brown,
Hide in a green and furry skin,
While April shakes her robins down,
And dogwood disappears in lace --
I scratch my head and wonder then
Whether with miracles commonplace,
One will occur in the hearts of men,
Or must a tree bear Christ again?

                ———
      Ladies' Home Journal, April 1950, p. 226

My Love and I

My love lives in a cottage high
Upon the forehead of a hill.
Beneath her in the valleys lie
The giant winds asleep and still.
Above her in the winter air
The battlemented clouds are piled.
My love is innocent and fair
And vulnerable as a child.

And if I were a god, I'd take
My love into my arms and hold
Her safe from any winds that wake,
Secure from winter's iron cold.
But I am but her counterpart,
Made of the selfsame fragile stuff.
I can but hold her in my heart
And pray it may prove strong enough.

The Saturday Evening Post, Jan. 3, 1953, p.45

Requiem

Now that you are gone and sorrow
Waits tomorrow and tomorrow
And for all tomorrows after
Empty both of tears and laughter,
I shall move in sightless space,
Void of orbit or of place,
Praying that we somehow might
Find each other in the night.
Now that what is done is done,
Faith shall be my only sun,
God a promise like a star
Rising in the hope that far
From these boundaries of men
We may meet and love again.

———

The Saturday Evening Post, Oct. 19, 1957, p. 100

Sky Cottage

Hard by the edge of earth, along the shore
Of sky itself I lived with my true love,
Where winds came foaming up the valley floor
Or broke in clouds upon the blue above.
It was a foolish place for us to be,
Two lovers on the brink of all that far
Illimitable waste of restless sea
That touched at once our cottage and a star.
We had no wall, no dike, to hold it back,
No boat to reach the highlands of the sun,
And when the night came rising, cold and black,
Our days together were suddenly done,
And I was left upon the beach of dawn,
Searching, bewildered, where my love had gone.

―――――

The Saturday Evening Post, July 25, 1959, p. 83

Search for the Sun

Once we could walk together, hand in hand,
Across a frozen world, all drifted white,
To better places in a greener land
Where April scattered golden coins of light.
We had each other. What more did we need
To travel safely through a bitter season,
When ice lay underfoot, as cruel as greed,
And sleet attached the heart without a reason?
But now the promises of singing birds
Awakens only memories of spring,
I cannot find the sun or barter words
Of sorrow for a leaf or robin wing,
And though I know I must be somehow wrong,
The winter seems to hold me all year long.

The Saturday Evening Post, April 23, 1960, p.120

Alone Awake

I waken in the wilderness of night
Where shadows move about a burning moon,
And all my thoughts fly upward to its light,
Moth-like and futile. I shall weary soon
And close my eyes again and try to sleep.
For I'll not find you here, my love, though I
Have searched the black shores and the flow of deep
Blue darkness in the river of the sky.
Oh, I have been deceived a time or two:
Once when a flight of stars before the dawn
Hovered like golden birds, I turned to you,
Sharing their loveliness, but you were gone.
And for me there were no more singing stars,
Only my heart that fluttered at its bars.

―――――

The Saturday Evening Post, May 23, 1959

Acceptance

I have, perhaps, loved overmuch
The place, the person and the day,
And cannot now abide the touch
Of time that takes them all away.
I have, perhaps, tried overhard
To bind quicksilver moments fast,
Stubborn enough to disregard
That nothing here can ever last.
I cannot catch the falling star
Nor cup the fire in my hand,
Forbid the wintertime or bar
The tide from covering the sand,
And I have learned at bitter cost
No man can find what he has lost.

      The Saturday Evening Post

Timber Patch

I've chopped away at trees enough
To know that some are soft inside,
And some, like ironwood, are tough
In bone and gristle, heart and hide.

Shagbark hickory spills its blood
Easy as a bright vein flowing;
Black-gum tree and willow wood
Heal the cut and keep on growing.

If a knife edge girdles beech,
One short summer sucks it dry;
But sycamore and sumac each
Scar the wound and scorn to die.

I'd give my ax away to know
What spirit breathes the magic breath
That forces one hurt tree to grow
And lets another bleed to death.

———

The Saturday Evening Post, July 7, 1951, p. 86

Old Earth

The earth and I have come to be
A mutually dependent pair.
He holds me up, and, as for me,
I scratch his back with my plowshare.

We jog along from year to year,
Summer to snow without an end,
But lately I begin to fear
Old age is troubling my friend.

He cannot bear my weight so well:
I totter down the garden rows.
Oh, he is failing, I can tell,
And I shall miss him when he goes.

―――――

                The Saturday Evening Post

Queen's Gambit Refused

All the tumbling waste of sea
Could wander like a river through
The space between this land of me
And that far distant shore of you.
I am a stony sort of place,
Years to the north of where you are.
The rocks are scarred by many a trace
Of glaciers, and the coldest star
Serves as a candle for my need.
But you are a night of amber moon,
Of lotus leaf and poppy seed,
A morning like a golden spoon
Spilling the sun. And so, my dear,
Let us remain—you there, me here.

The Saturday Evening Post, September 5, 1959

A Stony Field

When my years stood at just a score,
I gave my belt a hitch and curled
My fingers on the plow and swore
To carve a furrow round the world.

I hadn't counted on the stones,
The multitudes of rooted rocks,
Nor on the stiffness of the bones
That comes from calendars and clocks.

Today upon my patch of sod
I hitch my pants up as before
And breathe a word of thanks to God
That I don't own an acre more.

―――

The Saturday Evening Post, May 18, 1957, p.58

Pear Tree

I never can persuade my tree to bear
The ripe, bell-bottomed, yellow sort of pear
That shines in autumn in the grocery store,
Cool and honey-sweet from skin to core.
I guess, like cattle, pears reflect the stock;
My tree has sucked its nourishment from rock
Three generations that I know about.
Small wonder that the pears, when they come out,
Are wizened, bitter lumps of granite, hung
On crooked boughs, bird-eaten and bee-stung.
And for two cents I'd chop it down, but then
I'd never see it blossom white again.

The Saturday Evening Post, April 30, 1949, p.134

Unwilling Traveler

Reluctantly I walk, with many a look
Over my shoulder at the sun. It took
The calendar itself to make me go
Plodding up this path to ice and snow.
Oh, I'll admit the scene is fair to see,
With glory nesting in the maple tree
And every leaf a shining gold doubloon,
And every night brimful of harvest moon.
But I have come to learn it's not the view
That matters much, but where the road leads to,
And if I could, I'd pitch a tent right here
Where autumn still is in the shock and ear;
Or, better yet, I'd turn around and run
Straight back into the lap of summer sun.

―――

The Saturday Evening Post, Oct. 10, 1959, p.68

High Swallow

When shadows get up on their hands and knees
And summer dark begins to rise,
Its black arms full of fireflies
To scatter in the locust trees,
The lark goes early off to bed,
The sun-warmed earth against his breast;
The drowsy robin hides his head
As soon as dusk brims up his nest.

But swallows climb on pointed wings
Up cliffs of darkness toward the light.
They scale the mountain of the night,
The last of soaring, shining things.
Their silver scissors catch the sun
And make all earth-bound creatures turn
Gray faces upward, one by one,
Toward heaven to watch the bright birds burn.

―――――

The Saturday Evening Post, June 28, 1952, p.46

Moss Hartman

Moss Hartman is as good a man as you.
He mixes farming in the best he can
With fishing, hunting, raising dogs that do
Run musical at night. No better man
Than Moss for sitting round a winter fire
And telling dog from dog by different bay,
Or knowing when the fox begins to tire
From hearing hounds bell out a mile away.
Moss Hartman is a knowing man. I've seen
Him shooting ringnecks, never wasting shot,
And taking trout from riffles white and green.
Moss can do anything, as like as not.
And it's a dirty business, you'll admit,
To take his farm because he owes a bit.

―――

Prairie Schooner

Winter Thunder

You have no right up there. Can't you remember
This time of year is out-of-bounds for thunder?
What business have you here in mid-December
Growling over midnight bones, I wonder.
Startling gully-washers down the creeks
And rattling the winter stars together,
You roll your yellow eyes and puff your cheeks
And blow the night wide open with March weather.
Well, that's the way it goes. A fellow gets
A set of fixed ideas he can rely on,
And then along comes something that upsets
His apple cart and dumps a dripping sky on
Top of him to leave him at a loss
And let him understand, I guess, who's boss.

The Saturday Evening Post

Snow Fire

My eyes are dazzled by the white
Glitter of the winter light,
Hard as ice and cold as hate
And scoured bright as armor plate.
The ridge is flaming in the sun,
The fields are burning, every one,
And all about, above, below,
Blaze the diamonds of the snow.
But now the clouds of crimson fire
Smolder down like old desire,
And embers of the daylight die
To silver ashes in a sky
As soft as half-remembered sorrow,
Till the kindling of tomorrow.

The Saturday Evening Post

The Search

I had a dream once of a place
Where I would give my heart to be:
Sunlight was there and tall green hills
And ever the sound of sea.

So I set out to search the edge
Of all the oceans in the world
And left footprints in yellow sand
Wherever white waves curled.

And I shall wander till I'm old,
Follow my dream and never swerve,
Knowing the quest itself is more
Than likely I deserve.

The Magic Patch

My Aunt May's garden plot was all her own.
She dug it up in spring and raked it fine
And planted seeds and tended it alone
With trowel and hoe and water can. Each vine
Each plant, each root, each stalk, with loving words
And tender hands she wooed. She put to flight
The hen, the goose, the dog, the boys and birds,
And served it on her knees, earth's acolyte.
Then came a day of blue and golden weather,
At just the right conjunction of the stars,
When all the garden grew was brought together
And bottled up in glittering green jars:
A kind of magic that, when she was done,
Tasted the winter through of summer sun.

A Special Joy

A singularly dank and sodden day
Broods in a litter of falls discarded trash,
A crumple of worn-out leaves, a sky as gray
As an old man's tired grief, as gray as ash.
Beyond my weather-spotted windowpane
The garden sprawls, a wreck on winter's reef,
All broken stalk and stubble, a cold rain
Lashing against it, with a single leaf
Dangling from the quince tree and, behold,
One quince suspended like a ball of gold.

Oh, yellow, hard, unlovely, bitter fruit,
Unwanted and unsung, thou hast not been
My special joy, thou lump of ill repute,
Thou squirt of acid pouched in leather skin.
But I forgive thee now the puckered mouth,
The outraged palate and the withered tongue.
Thou art my little sun, my touch of South,
My remnant of July forever young,
And I shall venture out and gather thee
To hang in triumph on my Christmas tree.

The Coming In

At sundown when the shadows lie
Like giants on the valley floor
And ridgetops burn along the sky,
The cows come in to stand before
The crimson barn; their patient eyes
Pray to the door to be let in.
The horses in a net of flies
Stamp and shrug their dappled skin.
The hens squat in a bumpy row
Along the roost, and here a pair
Of homeward limping hound dogs go
With tick in ear and bur in hair,
While overhead barn swallows sew
Seams in the honey-colored air.

The Saturday Evening Post, August 12, 1950, p.46

Rock Ridge Elegy

Just at his line the rocks began,
His fields were cobbled up with stones,
Across his earth the ridges ran
And mountains lifted old gray bones.

His profits and his soil were thin,
With little lard on land or stock,
But hard of purpose, hard of chin,
He fought the farm and piled the rock.

As stubborn as a cocklebur
And tougher than a hickory limb,
He cleared the fields of stone before
They set this handsome stone on him.

Music Lover

O'Brien built his shack and stayed
Between the mountains and the bogs,
Where blackbirds piped a serenade
And every evening cellos played,
Plucked by a thousand frogs.

The rain fell down and rarely stopped,
The mountains sent them bears,
And in the moonlight rabbits hopped
About his garden rows and cropped
His vegetables on shares.

"Why do you stay, O'Brien lad,
Between the bogs and the mountains?
Mosquitoes here are very bad
And rain alone will drive you mad
With its eternal fountains."

"I do not know, the point is moot,
The bears are poor playfellows,
The rabbits rob me leaf and root.
It must be that I love the flute
And have an ear for cellos."

Star Lost

The child was busy in the sand,
Soberly heaping up a hill
Or scooping with a tiny hand
A hollow for the sea to fill.

She waded by the ebbing tide
And almost trod upon a star,
Fallen somehow there beside
The ocean stretching green and far.

But even as she bent to reach
Her hands out for the mystery,
A wave came sweeping up the beach
And took the star into the sea.

So I sat by her in the sun
And dried her tears and hushed her lips
And told her how the stars had run
Forever from my fingertips.

Gray Lace

By some strange miracle of grace
We have a world beneath our feet,
Love to warm us, food to eat,
And heaven arched above this place.
But being human, we remember
Faces we have loved before
And days that can return no more
From some far-off and lost November.
So let this day keep its slow pace
And step serene from east to west,
Its quiet hours softly dressed
In earth's brown velvet, sky's gray lace,
And let us not forget to vow
Our thanks for then as well as now.

The Saturday Evening Post, Nov. 26, 1949, p.89

Sergeant Herbert Merrill

Circa 1944

Herbert James Merrill
(1915-1995)

Born in Chicago, Merrill was to the Midwest what Robert Frost was to New England. His hundreds of published poems, mostly sonnets, evoke a more innocent era steeped in hard-scrabble naturalism. His philosophy, while hinting at optimism in the cycling seasons of nature, is also edgy with uncertainty. His often-folksy characters are more rough-hewn than sentimental.

Merrill was a professor of English Literature and creative writing at Wittenberg University in Springfield, Ohio, for more than twenty-five years. He attended Northwestern University and received his doctorate from Indiana University where he taught before moving to Springfield.

He was a cartoonist, penned short stories and a couple of novels, but was best known for his poems in *The Saturday Evening Post, Prairie Schooner, Ladies' Home Journal, The Atlantic Monthly*, and several other national magazines.

Merrill has received many awards including *The Sparrowgrass Poetry Forum's* Distinguished Poet

Award for "Fact Finding," which was included in *Treasured Poems of America* right before his death.

Made in the USA
Monee, IL
17 June 2023